2017 *Weird & Wacky* 9th Edition
HOLIDAY MARKETING GUIDE
Your business marketing calendar of ideas

Ginger Marks

DocUmeant *Publishing*
244 5th Avenue
Suite G-200
NY, NY 10001
646-233-4366
www.DocUmeantPublishing.com

Volume 9 First Edition, December 2016

Published by DocUmeant Publishing
244 5th Ave, Ste G–200
NY, NY 10001

646-233-4366

Editor Wendy VanHatten
VanHatten Writing Services

www.wendyvanhatten.com

Layout & Design Ginger Marks
DocUmeant Designs

www.DocUmeantDesigns.com

ISBN: 978-1-937801-76-2

Praise for the Weird & Wacky Holiday Marketing Guide through the years ...

"*Ginger has created a clever and fascinating resource for you to stand out from the rest. If you are looking to truly make a positive impression, use this book now!*" — **Peggy McColl,** New York Times Best-Selling Author (2016 Edition)

"*I absolutely love this! Creating a marketing plan takes work, and this calendar makes it so much easier. This is a 'MUST-HAVE' tool for every author and entrepreneur!*" —**Ellen Violette,** Award-Winning Publishing & Platform Building Coach, 6 Time #1 Best-Selling Author & Grammy-nominated Songwriter, www.theebookcoach.com (2016 Edition)

"*People love to buy. They especially love to buy when they have a reason. The* **Holiday Marketing Guide** *provides clever marketing strategies to increase sales every month of the year based on events and holidays. It's a brilliant guide for the savvy marketer.*" —**Daniel Hall,** Creator of *Free Marketing Tutorials* at DanielHallPresents.com (2016 Edition)

"*Ginger Marks has put together a fantastic resource! If you are looking for outside of the box ideas for marketing as well as for celebrating, you are going to love the Weird & Wacky Holiday Marketing Guide. As a former elementary school teacher I wish I had had a copy of this incredible resource when I was teaching. The month-long and week-long holidays, listed throughout this guide, could create the foundation for exciting study units.*" —**D'vorah Lansky, M.Ed.** Best-Selling author of *Book Marketing Made Easy,* www.BookMarketingMadeEasy.com (2016 Edition)

Contents

Foreword

Events are one of the smartest prescriptions for slumping sales and for maintaining a healthy business. It's not enough anymore to merely have goods on the shelf and open the doors on time every day. We all need to reinvent our businesses to keep them thriving and healthy. And, that is just what this book helps you achieve. This unique marketing book continues to win awards year after year and remains a #1 Best-Seller in the Business Marketing genre. Highly praised by marketing experts and now in its ninth edition, this book offers more fun and easy marketing ideas exclusively penned for the calendar year 2017. Now you can grow your business with strategies built around wacky holidays, observed throughout the world, for the entire 2017 calendar year. If you missed the premier 2009 issue or want to complete your collection, all previous and unique yearly editions are available at http://www.HolidayMarketingGuide.com.

As *Weird & Wacky Holiday Marketing Guide* is now read and used internationally I have decided to include International Independence Day listings and US State Fairs. In future editions, you will most likely find additional International holidays listed. However, for now, I thought I would get you used to seeing other countries represented with their respective Independence Day listings.

To take advantage of the information provided, pick a day and discover the unusual holidays celebrated on that date. Then, read the corresponding month's "Holiday Marketing Ideas" section to find a simple implementation or allow it to open your creative mind and think of some of your own.

Please note that the asterisk (*) in front of a holiday means a specific holiday is celebrated on that numerical date each year. For example, Christmas Day is December 25 no matter what day that falls on during the calendar week.

Here's another exceptional marketing idea for you I discovered when visiting BrownieLocks.com back in 2009, and which is now listed in the official *Chase Calendar of Events* which I cull from every year. Bonza Bottler Days™—the day is the same as the month it is in. That equates to: 1/1, 2/2, 3/3, etc. There is one in every month. There you have it; another extra fine excuse for an event to boost your notoriety and sales each and every month!

This is by no means a comprehensive edition. I have made all attempts to ensure the accuracy of the contents. If you encounter errors, or know of a holiday that needs to be included, please let me know so they can be addressed in future editions. But remember, if your suggested holiday addition is not listed in the official *Chase Calendar of Events* it is not eligible for inclusion.

Read on, have fun, initiate your own version of these holidays, and reap the benefit for your business.

Ginger Marks

P.S. I have included a 'Notes to Self' at the close of this book once again to assist in implementing your Weird & Wacky Holiday Marketing Plan events for 2017.

P.S.S. Introducing The *Weird & Wacky Holiday Marketing Companion Playbook*. This new tool is intended to help you to create, organize, and put the FUN back into your marketing plan. Each monthly calendar offers space for you to begin your planning and keep all your notes in one handy book. Since each year the physical calendar days rotate I have left the date numbers blank to enable you to make use of this *Companion Playbook* beginning today.

Annual Dates of Note

International Year of Sustainable Tourism for Development

The United Nations General Assembly has named 2017 the International Year of Sustainable Tourism for Development. The UN World Tourism Organization (WTO) is leading the initiative, collaborating with other relevant UN agencies, governments, organizations, and other stakeholders to celebrate and strengthen the link between sustainable tourism and international development.

The year seeks to highlight the many benefits of sustainable tourism, particularly for developing countries. The UN says tourism strengthens world peace by giving travelers greater understanding and appreciation for other cultures and heritages; it fosters economic growth by creating decent jobs and generating trade opportunities; it helps eradicate poverty by giving women and children economic power; and it does so in a way that is economically, socially, and environmentally sustainable.

Throughout this international year, countries are encouraged to support international tourism as a way to help developing nations flourish and to make sure their own tourism industries are sustainable.

For information contact UNWTO at omt@unwto.org or visit www2.unwto.org.

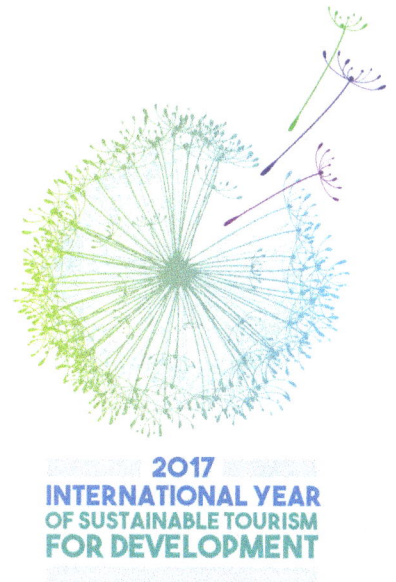

2017 INTERNATIONAL YEAR OF SUSTAINABLE TOURISM FOR DEVELOPMENT

International Year of Vaquita

The shy and beautiful vaquita (also known as a Gulf of California porpoise) is defined by extremes: it is the smallest whale (an adult is scarcely five feet long), it has the smallest habitat of any whale species — only at the northern end of the Gulf of California at the mouth of the Colorado River delta — and it is the most endangered whale species. In May 2016, the Mexican government released the most current population data for the vaquita, and it indicated that there were fewer than 60 individuals. Both because of its timidity and its low population numbers, few vaquita have been observed and so little is known about them.

Seeking to raise awareness of this porpoise and halt its slide into extinction, Whale Times, Ocean Coast Aquarium and Southwest Fisheries Science Center, NOAA Fisheries have designated 2017 the Year of the Vaquita. These organizations plan to educate the public about what they can do to help save this rare marine mammal and work with schools and other organizations to raise awareness to help save the remaining animals. For more information email: savethevaquita@whaletimes.org or visit www.whaletimes.org.

Chinese Year of the Rooster[1]

Rooster is the tenth in the 12-year cycle of Chinese zodiac sign. The Years of the Rooster include 1921, 1933, 1945, 1957, 1969, 1981, 1993, 2005, 2017, 2029...

The rooster is almost the epitome of fidelity and punctuality. For ancestors who had no alarm clocks, the crowing was significant, as it could awaken people to get up and start to work. In Chinese culture, another symbolic meaning the chicken carries is exorcising evil spirits.

People born in the Year of Rooster according to Chinese zodiac have many excellent characteristics, such as being honest, bright, communicative and ambitious. Most of them are born pretty or handsome, and prefer to dress up. In daily life, they seldom rely on others. However, they might be enthusiastic about something quickly, but soon be impassive. Thus, they need to have enough faith and patience to insist on one thing.

Strengths

Independent, capable, warm-hearted, self-respect, quick minded.

Weaknesses

Impatient, critical, eccentric, narrow-minded, selfish.

Matches

Perfect: Ox, Snake

If combining with people in Ox or Snake signs, most of them will obtain everlasting and harmonious marriage lives. The connection between them can become tight. In addition, couples of these combinations always become enviable ones in other people's eyes.

Avoid: Rat, Rabbit, Horse, Rooster, Dog

They have a large chance to obtain a tough and unstable love life if they get married to people with the above five signs. During their whole life, they always meet difficulties and troubles. However, they don't have enough abilities to solve them because of their born different opinions and attitudes with each other. Lots of divergences will damage the relationship finally.

Rooster's Personality by Blood Type

Blood Type O: Most of them are clever and wise. They can always find the fastest way to learn new things and adapt to new environment.

Blood Type A: They are gentle, generous, and kind-hearted in ordinary life. Thus, they always win high popularity among surrounding people.

Blood Type B: Type B people have keen insight when they need to make decisions. They are suitable for being the group leader because they usually can provide valuable suggestions.

Blood Type AB: They have outstanding working abilities that can easily attract others' attention. Most of them are willing to help others even though they have more important things to do.

---

1   Travel China Guide. http://www.travelchinaguide.com/intro/social_customs/zodiac/rooster.htm.

JANUARY

MONTH-LONG HOLIDAYS

Jan 6 – Feb 28 Carnival Season
Jan 7 – Feb 9 Germany: Munich Fashing Carnival

Be Kind to Food Servers Month, Book Blitz Month, Get Organized Month, International Brain Teaser Month, International Child-Centered Divorce Month, International Creativity Month, International New Year's Resolutions Month for Business, National Clean Up Your Computer Month, National Glaucoma Awareness Month, National Hot Tea Month, National Mentoring Month, National Personal Self-Defense Awareness Month, National Poverty in America Awareness Month, National Radon Action Month, National skating Month, National Slavery and Human Trafficking Prevention Month, National Stalking Awareness Month, National Volunteer Blood Donor Month, Oatmeal Month, Shape Us Up Month, Teen Driving Awareness Month, Worldwide Rising Star Month

WEEK-LONG HOLIDAYS

Jan 1 – 3 Japanese Era New Year

Jan 1 – 7 Diet Resolution Week

Jan 1 – 8 New Year's Resolution Week

Jan 2 – 8 Someday We'll Laugh about This Week

Jan 8 – 14 Dating & Life Coach Recognition Week, Home Office Safety and Security Week

Jan 11-17 Cuckoo Dancing Week

Jan 13 – 15 Art Deco Weekend, Vegaspex

Jan 16 – 20 Healthy Weight Week, Sugar Awareness Week

Jan 16 – 22 Career Builder Challenge

Jan 21 – 22 Bald Eagle Appreciation Day

Jan 22 – 28 International Handwriting Analysis Week

Jan 22 – 29 Clean Out Your Inbox Week

Jan 29 – Feb 4 Catholic Schools Week

DAILY HOLIDAYS

1. Betsy Ross Birthday (1752), *Bonza Bottler Day™, Canada: Polar Bear Swim, *Copyright Revision Law Signed (1976), Cuba: Liberation Day & Anniversary of the Revolution, Czech–Slovak Divorce (1993; Anniversary of separation into two nations), *Ellis Island Opened Anniversary (125th Anniversary), *Emancipation Proclamation (1863), *Euro Introduced (1999), *First Baby Boomer Born–Kathleen Casey

Wilkens in Philadelphia, PA (1946), *Haiti: Independence Day, Kim Philby Birthday (1912), *Mummer's Parade, *National Environmental Policy Act (1970), *New Year's Day, *New Year's Dishonor List Day, Paul Revere Birthday (1735), Saint Basil's Day, Stock Exchange Holiday, *Z–Day

2. 55 MPH Speed Limit Day (1974), Haiti: Ancestor's Day, *Happy Mew Year for Cats Day, Japan: Kakizome, Switzerland: Berchtoldstag

3. *Alaska Admission Day, Congress Assembles, *Drinking Straw Day (1888), Memento Mori Day, Saint Genevieve Day

4. *Amnesty for Polygamists: Anniversary (1893), *Dimpled Chad Day, Earth at Perihelion, *Elizabeth Ann Bayley–Seton Day, *Pop Music Chart Day, Sir Isaac Newton Birthday (1643), *Trivia Day, *World Braille Day, World's Tallest Building Day

5. *Alvin Ailey (1931), *Five-Dollar-a-Day Minimum Wage Day (1914), Twelfth Night

6. *Armenian Christmas, *Epiphany or Twelfth Day, Italy: La Befana, Pan Am Circles Earth (75th Anniversary), *Three Kings Day

7. *First Balloon Fight Across English Channel (1785), *Harlem Globetrotter's Day, *International Programmers' Day, Japan: Nanakusa & Usokae, Orthodox Christmas, Trans-Atlantic Phoning (90th Anniversary)

8. Argyle Day, Asarrah B'Tevet, *Elvis Presley Birth (1935), *Midwife's Day or Women's Day, *National Joygerm Day, *Show and Tell Day at Work, Switzerland: Meitlisunntig, *War on Poverty Day (1964)

9. *Aviation In America Day (1793), Japan: Coming of Age Day, *Panama's Martyr Day, Plough Monday, National Clean Off Your Desk Day, National Thank God it's Monday! Day, Switzerland: Meitlinsunntig

10. Poetry at Work Day

11. Learn Your Name in Morse Code Day

12. *Haiti Earthquake Day (2010), National Hot Yea Day, *Women Denied Vote (1915)

13. Blame Someone Else Day, Friday the Thirteenth, Norway: Tyvendedagen, *Radio Broadcasting Day, Russia: Old New Year's Eve, Sweden: Saint Knut's Day

14. *Benedict Arnold Day, Eagle Days, *Ratification Day

15. Molière Day, Stephen Foster Day

16. *Appreciate a Dragon Day, *Civil Service Day, Japan: Haru-No-Yabuiri, *National Nothing Day, *Religious Freedom Day

17. *Al Capone Day, *Cable Car Day, *Ben Franklin Birthday (1706), *Judgment Day, Kid Inventors' Day, Quarterly Estimated Federal Income Tax Payers' Due Date (also Apr 15, Jun 15 and Sep 15, 2015), Rid the World of Fad Diets and Gimmicks Day, Saint Anthony's Day, Southern California Earthquake Day

18. *Louis and Clark Expedition Commissioned (1803), *Pooh Day

19. *Confederate Heroes Day (Texas), Ethiopia: Timket, Get to Know Your Customers Day (also April 20, July 20, and Oct 19, set aside to get to know your customers even better), Poe Day, *Tin Can Day

20. Arbor Day in Florida, Brazil: San Sebastian's Day, Inauguration Day, International Fetish Day, Women's Healthy Weight Day

21. First Concorde Flight, Kiwanis International: Anniversary, *National Hugging Day™

22. *Answer Your Cat's Questions Day, *Roe vs. Wade Day, *Saint Vincent Feast Day

23. *National Handwriting Day, National Pie Day, Snowplow Mailbox Hockey Day

24. *Belly Laugh Day, *Beer Can Day, *National Compliment Day

25. *A Room of One's Own Day, First Scheduled Transcontinental Flight, *Macintosh Computer Day (1984), Saint Dwynwen Day

26. Australia: Australia Day, Dental Drill Day, Dominican Republic: National Holiday, India: Republic Day

27. Apollo I: Spacecraft Fire: 50th Anniversary, Germany: Day of Remembrance for Victims of Nazism, *Mozart Day, National Geographic Society Day, National Preschool Fitness Day, *Thomas Crapper Day, United Nations: International Day of Commemoration in Memory of the Victims of the Holocaust, *Viet Nam Peace Day

28. *Challenger Space Shuttle Explosion (1986), Chinese New Year, Data Privacy Day, Local Quilt Shop Day, National Seed Swap Day

29. Curmudgeons Day, *Seeing Eye Dog Day, World Leprosy Day

30. Blood Sunday, Bubble Wrap Appreciation Day,*Inane Answering Message Day, Tet Offensive Begins: Anniversary

31. First Social Security Check Issued Day, *Inspire Your Heart with Art Day, Nauru: National Holiday, Schubert Day

HOLIDAY MARKETING IDEAS FOR JANUARY

Worldwide Rising Star Month — This month's feature lends well to coaching, training, and presentations. However, don't stop there! Something that I immediately thought about is getting together several organizations throughout the month to visit nursing homes and AFLs. Shower the residents with pins made up to celebrate them. They could read, "Worldwide Rising Star!" Or perhaps give small gifts. Your time and talent given to share with those whom most often get set aside and forgotten will be much appreciated. And, not only appreciated by the facility and residents, but you'll be a media darling as well. So, don't forget to let them know what you have planned through the month of January. See the Appendix for sample stickers or pins.

Jan 4 World's Tallest Building Day — Today is the day we look to the skies. Building each other up through training and simple acts of kindness and gratitude can do a lot for building your bottom line. Think of things you can do to be helpful to your customers and clients that will greatly impact their lives. The easiest thing to do is to send them a card or a note. Getting into the height of the issue could include training or storytelling. The sky's the limit!

Jan 7 Transatlantic Phoning — In today's global economy, we often find ourselves connecting with people near and far. To celebrate that fact, we focus on the advancement of international communications. Perhaps you sell communications equipment or services. Then again, you might be a communications coach. Either of these career professionals should make note of this holiday made just for them. Super ways for the rest of us to use this holiday are by connecting on Skype or a webinar service and have a party of sorts.

Burj Khalifa.© Donaldytong

Jan 13 Friday the Thirteenth — Whether you believe Friday the 13th brings good luck or bad this special day only comes around ever-so-often. Here's an explanation courtesy of Wikipedia: Each Gregorian 400-year cycle contains 146,097 days (365 × 400 = 146,000 normal days, plus 97 leap days). 146,097 ÷ 7 = 20,871 weeks. Thus, each cycle contains the same pattern of days of the week (and thus the same pattern of Fridays that are on the 13th). The 13th day of the month is slightly more likely to be a Friday than any other day of the week.[20] On average, there is a Friday the 13th once every 212.35 days (compared to Thursday the 13th, which occurs only once every 213.59 days).

This one's for genuine sufferers of Triskaidekaphobia or paraskevidekatriaphobia, or fear of Friday the 13th. An anxiety disorders researcher at Rutgers University notes that "one study estimates that $800 to $900 million is lost in business on Friday the 13th because people stay home from work, refuse to fly or engage in routine business." So, make this your lucky day. While all those folks are sitting at home, have a shopping party on-line! If you opt for an in-person party, why not try theme shaped ice-cubes and skeleton pretzels? Check the appendix for instructions.

Jan 24 Beer Can Day — Whether you love beer or not, you can highlight your business if you align it with a restaurant that features this livacious brew. Say, for every beer ordered the restaurant will match your, say, 25-cent donation. Find a worthy cause to donate to and let the media know what you are up to.

Alternatively, you might entertain the idea of beer tasting at a local brewery or merely handing out beer can shaped Happy Beer Can Day cards with your business prominently displayed. And, don't forget to blog about Beer Can Day on your blog.

FEBRUARY

MONTH-LONG HOLIDAYS

AMD/Low Vision Awareness Month, *American Heart Month, Bake for Family Fun Month, Beat the Heat Month, Festival of the North Month, International Boost Self-Esteem Month, Library Lovers Month, Marfan Syndrome Awareness Month, National African American History Month, National Bird-Feeding Month, National Black History Month, National Cherry Month, National Condom Month, National Mend A Broken Heart Month, National Parent Leadership Month, National Pet Dental Health Month, National Teen Dating Violence Awareness and Prevention Month, National Time Management Month, Plant the Seeds of Greatness Month, Return Shopping Carts to the Supermarket Month, Spay/Neuter Awareness Month, Spunky Old Broads Month, Wise Health Care Consumer Month, Worldwide Renaissance of the Heart Month, Youth Leadership Month

WEEK-LONG HOLIDAYS

Feb 3 – 20 Canada: Winterlude

Feb 5 – 11 Children's Authors and Illustrators Week, Dump Your Significant Jerk Week, Freelance Writers Appreciation Week

Feb 6 – 10 International Networking Week

Feb 8 – 11 Association of Writers and Writing Programs Conference and Book fair (Washington, D. C.)

Feb 8 – 14 Love Makes the World Go Round; but, Laughter Keeps Us from Getting Dizzy Week

Feb 10 – 12 Gold Rush Days

Feb 12 – 18 International Flirting Week, Random Acts of Kindness Week

Feb 13 – 19 Love a Mensch Week

Feb 14 – 15 Wings Over the Platte Spring Migration Celebration

Feb 14 – 16 World AG Expo

Feb 16 – 19 Learning Disabilities Association of American International Conference (Baltimore)

Feb 16 – 20 American Association for the Advancement of Science Annual Meeting (Boston)

Feb 17 – 20 Great Backyard Bird Count

Feb 19 – 25 Build a Better Trade Show Image Week, National Eating Disorders Awareness Week, National Engineers Week

Feb 24 – 25 Texas Cowboy Poetry Gathering Days

Feb 26 – 28 Shrovetide

Feb 26 – Mar 4 Telecommuter Appreciation Week

Feb 27 – 28 Fasching

Feb 27 – Apr 7 Lent

DAILY HOLIDAYS

1. Car Insurance Day, Freedom Day, G. I. Joe Day, National Candy-Making Day, National Girls and Women in Sports Day, National Signing Day, *Robinson Crusoe Day

2. *Bonza Bottler Day™, *Candelmas, *Groundhog Day, *Hedgehog Day, *Imbolic Sled Dog Day, Mexico: Dia de la Candelaria, The Record of a Sneeze Day

3. Bubble Gum Day, *Four Chaplains Memorial Day, *The Day The Music Died Day (1959), *Income Tax Birthday, Japan: Bean Throwing Festival Day (Setsubun), National Wear Red Day, Vietnam: National Holiday, Working Naked Day

4. *Facebook Launch Day (2004), Lindbergh Day, Medjool Date Day, National Barber Day, *Rosa Parks Birthday (1913), Sri Lanka:Independence Day, Take Your Child to the Library Day, *USO Day, World Cancer Day

5. England: Grimaldi Memorial Service/Clown Church Service, *Family Leave Bill (1993), Longest War in History Ends (1985), Mexico: Constitution Day, Move Hollywood & Broadway to Lebanon, Switzerland: Homstrom, *Weatherperson's Day

6. Accession of Queen Elizabeth II (65th Anniversary), New Zealand: Waitangi Day, United Nations: International Day of Zero Tolerance for Female Genital Mutilation

7. African–American Coaches Day, *Ballet Day, *Chaplin's "Tramp" Day (1914), *Charles Dickens (1812), Granada: Independence Day, National Black HIV/AIDS Awareness Day, *Wave All Your Fingers At Your Neighbor's Day

8. *Boy Scouts of America Day (1910), Japan: Ha-Ri-Ku-Yo (Needle Mass), Opera Debut in the Colonies Day (1735), Slovenia: Culture Day

9. *Ernest Tubb (1914), *Gypsy Rose Lee (1914), Lebanon: St. Maron's Day, Read in a Bathtub Day, Union Officers Escape Libby Prison (1864)

10. *"All the News that's Fit to Print" Day, *Charles Lamb (1775), *First Computer Chess Victory over Human (1996), *First WWII Medal of Honor (1942), *Plimsoll Day, Treaty of Paris (1763)

11. Cameroon: Youth Day, China, Taiwan, Korea: Lantern Festival, *First Woman Episcopal Bishop (1989), Get Out Your Guitar Day, *Japan: National Foundation Day, Mandela Released Day (1990), *National Shut-in Visitation Day, *Pro Sports Wives Day, *Satisfied Staying Single Day, *Thomas Alva Edison Birthday (1847), Tu B'Shvat, *White Shirt Day

12. *Darwin Day, *Dracula Day, *Abraham Lincoln (1809) & Birthplace Cabin Wreath Laying Day, Man Day, Myanmar: Union Day, NAACP Day (1909), *Oglethorpe Day, *Safetypup's® Day

13. *Employee Legal Awareness Day, *First Magazine Published (1741), *Get a Different Name Day, *Madly In Love With Me Day, World Radio Day, National Wingman's Day

14. ENIAC Computer Day, *Ferris Wheel Day, *First Presidential Photograph Day (1849), *League of Women Voters Day, National Donor Day, *National Have-a-Heart Day, New Mexico: Extraterrestrial Culture Day, Race Relations Day, *Saint Valentine's Day

15. Afghanistan: Soviet Troop Withdrawal (1989), Asteroid Near Miss Day, Canada: Family Day & Maple Leaf Flag Day, *Galileo, Galilei (1564), *Lupercalia, *Remember the Maine Day, *Susan B. Anthony Day

16. Lithuania: Independence Day

17. *League of United Latin American Citizens (LULAC) Founded (1929), *My Way Day, *National PTA Founders Day, Random Acts of Kindness Day

18. Gambia: Independence Day, Helen Gurley Brown Day, Nepal: National Democracy Day, *Pluto (Planet) Day, World Whale Day

19. *Japanese Internment Day

20. Ansel Adams Day (1925), Canada: Family Day (Selected Provinces), Closest Approach of a Comet to Earth (1941), *Northern Hemisphere Hoodie Hoo Day (At high noon everyone yells "HoodiE-Hoo" to chase away winter and make way for spring.), Presidents' Day, *United Nations: World Day for Social Justice

21. Bangladesh: Martyrs Day, Erma Bombeck Day (1927), CIA Agent Arrested as Spy Day (1994), Travel Africa Day, *United Nations: International Mother Language Day, *Washington Monument Dedicated (1885)

22. *George Washington's Birthday (1732), Inconvenience Yourself™ Day, Montgomery Boycott Arrests Day (1956), Saint Lucia: Independence Day

23. Brunei Darussalam: National Day, *Curling is Cool Day, Diesel Engine Day, Discovere Girl Day, First Cloning of an Adult Animal (1997), Guyana: Anniversary of Republic, *Iwo Jima Day (flag raised), National Chili Day, Russia: Defender of the Fatherland Day, Single Tasking Day

24. Estonia: Independence Day, Gregorian Calendar Day (1582), Mexico: Flag Day, *Wilhelm Carl Grimm (1786), Steve Jobs Birthday (1955)

25. *Jim Backus Birthday (1913), Kuwait: National Day, Open That Bottle Night, World Sword Swallower's Day

26. Buffalo Bill Cody Day (1846), Daytona 500, Germany & Austria: Fasching Sunday, *Federal Communications Commission Created (FCC), (1934), *For Pete's Sake Day, Kuwait: Liberation Day, Orthodox Forgiveness Sunday (Cheesefare Sunday), *Levi Strauss Day

27. Dominican Republic: Independence Day, *Henry Wadsworth Longfellow Birthday (1807), Iceland: Bun Day, International Polar Bear Day, Orthodox Green Monday, Shrove Monday, Twenty-Second Amendment to US Constitution Ratification (1951)

28. Floral Design Day, Iceland: Bursting Day, International Pancake Day, Mardi Gras, *National Tooth Fairy Day, Paczki Day, Shrove Tuesday, Tiwain: Peace Memorial Day, World Spay Day

HOLIDAY MARKETING IDEAS FOR FEBRUARY

National Teen Dating Violence Awareness and Prevention Month — If you work with teens, this month is an important one, as you need to be aware of the impact events surrounding this holiday could make in their lives. Whether you are an author, counselor, doctor, or concerned parent, the events you host could be done at schools, clinics, churches, club houses, and many other venues. Then there are social media channels that teens flock to that would make for a superb venue. Think Twitter Chats, Facebook Groups, and even Google Hangouts. Teaching our young impressionable teens the right and wrong way to deal with their raging hormones when it comes to dating is of paramount importance.

Of note is that the official color for domestic violence is purple and the official color for dating abuse is orange. One very simple thing to do would be to have individuals or groups post photos on social media wearing whichever color is more appropriate for your group.

As with any other holiday, a flier, brochure, card, or other helpful pamphlet that provides information on this subject is the least you should do. Be sure to look in the appendix for tools and resources to assist you in this area. If you do host an event, be sure to let the media know. This is just the 'feel good' type of story news people crave.

Feb 3 Bubble Gum Day — Get out the Hubba Bubba, Bazooka® or your favorite stick gum. It's time to celebrate the awesomeness of this multigenerational pastime; chewing and blowing bubbles! According to Guinness World Records, Chad Fell (USA) blew a bubblegum bubble with a diameter of 50.8 cm (20 in) without using his hands at the Double Springs High School, Winston County, Alabama, USA on 24 April 2004.[2]

---

2   http://www.guinnessworldrecords.com/world-records/largest-bubblegum-bubble-blown

The secret of his success, says Chad, is blowing with three pieces of Dubble Bubble gum.

Feb 11 Get Out Your Guitar Day — Not just your guitar, but any instrument that has been relegated to your fond memories. It's time to get them out and strike up the band. If you are musically inclined, you should definitely celebrate this day. Have an open house and invite everyone you touch to bring their instrument of choice and make an evening of music together. Kazoo, rainstick, bag pipes, and all kinds of instruments, and yes your guitar, could make for a fun and entertaining time.

If music is not your forte, have an on-line event to remind your customers and clients to share their hidden dreams and air them. Alternatively, you could send them a 'note'. If you can do this by hand and snail mail it, you'll make a bigger impact than if you send an email. You'll find a sample note card cover in the appendix. Whatever way you decide to celebrate this Weird & Wacky Holiday, be sure to enjoy yourself doing so.

Feb 23 Discovere Girl Day — Formerly called Introduce a Girl to Engineering Day, this newly named holiday is set aside to remind us that the field of Engineering is not just for boys. Girls are encouraged to pursue their dreams and talents working in this formerly male dominated career path. So, today it would be a good idea to host or participate in events that challenge girls to go for their goals. This could be a life changing day for an enthusiastic young woman.

MARCH

MONTH-LONG HOLIDAYS

Mar 13 – Apr 15 Deaf History Month
Mar 1 – Apr 15 Lent
Mar 4 – 20 Iditarod Trail Sled Dog Race

Alport Syndrome Awareness Month, American Red Cross Month, Colorectal Cancer Awareness Month, Credit Education Month, Employee Spirit Month, Humorists Are Artists Month, International Ideas Month, International Listening Awareness Month, International Mirth Month, Irish-American Heritage Month, Mad for Plaid Month, Music in our Schools Month, National Clean Up Your IRS Act Month, National Colorectal Cancer Awareness Month (Different sponsor from Colorectal Cancer Awareness Month), National Craft Month, National Eye Donor Month, National Kidney Month, National Multiple Sclerosis Education and Awareness Month, National Nutrition Month®, National Peanut Month, National Umbrella Month, National Women's History Month, Optimism Month, Paws to Read Month, Play the Recorder Month, Poison Prevention Awareness Month, Red Cross Month, Save the Vaquita Month, Save Your Vision Month, Sing with Your Child Month, Social Work Month, Women's History Month, Workplace Eye Wellness Month, Youth Art Month

WEEK-LONG HOLIDAYS

Mar 1 – 7 National Cheerleading Week, Will Eisner Week

Mar 1 – 14 Japan: Omizutori (Water-Drawing Festival)

Mar 2 – 5 Emerald City Comicon

Mar 2 – 12 Florida Strawberry Festival

Mar 3 – 5 Aldo Leopold Weekend

Mar 3 – 7 CAMEX

Mar 3 – 12 England: Words by the Water: A Festival of Words and Ideas

Mar 5 – 11 Celebrate Your Name Week, National Consumer Protection Week, Professional Pet Sitters Week, Read an e-Book Week, Return the Borrowed Books Week, Teen Tech Week

Mar 6 – 10 National School Breakfast Week

Mar 8 – 15 HeForShe Arts Week

Mar 12 – 18 Camp Fire Birthday Week, Termite Awareness Week

Mar 13 – 19 Brain Awareness Week

Mar 14 – 16 London Book Fair

Mar 17 – 19 Sherlock Holmes Weekend

Mar 18 – 19 Military Through the Ages

Mar 19 – 25 National Animal Poison Prevention Week, World Folk Tales & Fables Week

Mar 20 – 26 Act Happy Week, United Kingdom: Shakespeare Week, Wellderly Week

Mar 21 – 27 United Nations: Week of Solidarity with the Peoples Struggling Against Racism and Racial Discrimination

Mar 24 – 26 American Crossword Puzzle Tournament

Mar 26 – Apr 1 National Protocol Officers' Week, Root Canal Awareness Week

Mar 27 – Apr 2 Mule Days

DAILY HOLIDAYS

1. Ash Wednesday, Bosnia & Herzegovina: Independence Day, *Iceland: Beer Day, Korea: Samiljol or Independence Movement Day, Korea: Samiljol or Independence Movement Day, National Black Women in Jazz and the Arts Day, National Horse Protection Day, *National Pig Day, Paraguay: National Heroes' Day, *Peace Corps Founded (1961), Plan a Solo Vacation Day, *Refired, Not Retired Day, Switzerland: Chalandrea Maraz, Wales: Saint David's Day, World Compliment Day, Zero Discrimination Day

2. Ethiopia: Adwa Day, *Dr Seuss Day, *Highway Numbers Day, *King Kong Premier (1933), NEA's Read Across America Day, United Kingdom & Ireland: World Book Day

3. Alexander Graham Bell (1847), *Bonza Bottler Day™, Bulgaria: Liberation Day, Dress in Blue Day, International Ear Care Day, Japan: Hina Matsuri (Doll Festival), Malawi: Martyr's Day, *National Anthem Day (1931), National Day of Unplugging, Shabbat across America and Canada, United Nations: World Wildlife Day, *What If Cats and Dogs Had Opposable Thumbs Day, World Day of Prayer

4. *National Grammar Day, Old Inauguration Day

5. Luxembourg: Bürgsonndeg, Namesake Day, National Poutine Day, Saint Piran's Day, Unites States Bank Holiday

6. Australia: Eight Hour Day or Labor Day, *Dred Scott Day, Fun Facts About Names Day, Ghana: Independence Day, Guam: Discovery Day or Magellan Day, *Michelangelo (1475)

7. Distinguished Service Medal Day, Peace Corp Day, Suez Canal Day, Town Meeting Day, Unique Names Day

8. Discover What Your Name Means Day, Panic Day, International Working Women's Day, National Proofreading Day, Registered Dietitian Nutritionists Day, Russia: International Women's Day, Syrian Arab Republic: Revolution Day, United Nations: International Women's Day, United States Income Tax (1913)

9. *Barbie Day, Belize: Baron Bliss Day, Name tag Day, Panic Day, Saint Frances of Rome: Feast Day, Ta'anit Ester, Vespucci Day, World Kidney Day

10. International Bagpipe Day, *Mario Day, Middle Name Pride Day, National Women and Girls HIV/AIDS Awareness Day, *Salvation Army Day, *Telephone Invention Day, *US Paper Money Day

11. Dream Day 2017, Genealogy Day, International Fanny Pack Day, *Johnny Appleseed Day, Lithuania: Restitution of Independence Day, National Urban Ballroom Dance Day

12. Check Your Batteries Day, Daylight Savings Time Begins, *FDR's First Fireside Chat (1933), Gabon: National Day, *Girl Scout Day, Moshoeshoe's Day, Mauritius: Independence Day, Purim, Spain: Fiesta de las Fallas

13. *Earmuffs Day, Fill Our Staplers Day (also Nov 6), Good Samaritan Involvement Day, National Open an Umbrella Indoors Day, Smart and Sexy Day, Commonwealth Day

14. *Albert Einstein Birthday (1879), Moth-er Day, Organize Your Home Office Day, Pi Day (as in the math pie = 3.14159265 etc.), 10 Most Wanted List Day

15. Brutus Day, Ides of March, True Confessions Day

16. Absolutely Incredible Kid Day, *Black Press Day (1827), Curlew Day, *Lips Appreciation Day, No Selfies Day

17. *Campfire USA Day, *Freedom of Information Day, Ireland: National Day, Saint Patrick's Day

18. Forgive Mom and Dad Day, *National Biodiesel Day, National Quilting Day, Play the Recorder Day, Save the Florida Panther Day

19. Saint Joseph's Day, Swallows Return to San Juan Capistrano Day, US Standard Time Act (1918), *Wyatt Earp (1848)

20. Australia: Canberra Day, *Great American Meat Out Day, Japan: Vernal Equinox Day, Kiss Your Fiancé Day, Maw-Ruz, Ostara, *Proposal Day®, Snowman Burning, Tunisia: Independence Day, *United Nations: International Day of Happiness, *Won't You Be My Neighbor Day

21. *Bach Day, *First Round-the-World Balloon Flight (1999), Iranian New Year: Noruz, Lesotho: National Tree Planting Day, Memory Day, Namibia: Independence Day, South Africa: Human Rights Day, *Twitter Day, *United Nations: International Day for the Elimination of Racial Discrimination, United Nations: International Day of Forests, United Nations: World Poetry Day, World Down Syndrome Day

22. As Young As You Feel Day, India: New Year's Day, *International Day of The Seal, *Louis L'Amour Day (1908), Laser Patented Day (1960), *National Goof-off Day, United Nations: World Day for Water (aka World Water Day)

23. Beat the Clock Day, "Big Bertha Paris Gun Day, *Liberty Day, National Puppy Day, National Tamale Day, *Near Miss Day, "OK" Day, *United Nations: World Meteorological Day

24. Argentina: National Day of Memory for Truth and Justice, Exxon Valdez Oil Spill (1989), *Houdini Day (1874), Philippine Independence, United Nations: International Day for the Right to the Truth Concerning Gross Human Rights Violations and for the Dignity of Victims, *World Tuberculosis Day

25. Be Mad Day, *Bed In for Peace Day, Earth Hour, *Greece: Greek Independence Day: National Day of Celebration of Greek & American Democracy, Maryland Day, National Medal of Honor Day, *Old New Year's Day, Pecan Day, Tolkien Reading Day, United Nations: International Day of Remembrance of The Victims of Slavery and The Transatlantic, United Nations: International Day of Solidarity with Detained and Missing Staff Members

26. Bangladesh: Independence Day, England: Mothering Sunday, European Union: Daylight Savings Time (Summertime begins), *Legal Assistants Day, *Make Up Your Own Holiday Day

27. *FDA Approves Viagra Day, *Quirky Country Music Song Titles Day, Seward's Day

28. American Diabetes Association Alert Day, Czech Republic: Teachers' Day

29. *Canada: British North America Act (1867), Central African Republic: Boganda Day, Dow Jones Day, *Knights of Columbus Founders Day, *National Mom & Pop Business Owner's Day, *Niagara Falls Runs Dry (1848), Taiwan: Youth Day, *Texas Loves The Children Day, Whole Grain Sampling Day

30. Anesthetic Day, *Doctors Day, Grass is Always Browner on the Other Side of the Fence Day, *Pencil Day, World Bipolar Day

31. *Bunsen Burner Day, Cesar Chavez Day, *Eiffel Tower Day (1998), International Hug a Medievalist Day, *National "She's Funny That Way" Day

HOLIDAY MARKETING IDEAS FOR MARCH

National Women's History Month — The whole month of March is a month to celebrate the affect women have had on history. Very few women were given any recognition at all throughout history, so those who did deserve to be remembered for their accomplishments. Nevertheless, what's to say we can't make some history of our own? This month, take the time to reflect on how you can make a difference in other's lives. Take the time to share your time and talents with those who could use a leg-up. Coaching programs and seminars are a great way to start. You can also do something much easier, by hand writing a note to thank those who have made a difference in your own business and life. Follow your heart and make a start to make an impact on someone else at every opportunity.

Mar 2 Highway Numbers Day — Without the numbers on our highways, we would easily get lost. There are not only numbered highways to ensure we get on the right one, but there are also those numbers at each exit to help us recognize when we get to our destinations. What memories mark the miles of your life? Are there special people who have helped you on your journey? Why not take the time to thank them? Sending a card or giving them a quick phone call is a terrific way to celebrate the milestones of your life.

If you ever wondered why we use numbers instead of names for highways, here's a website that will give you the specifics and quench your thirst for knowledge. Why, you might even consider creating a contest, tweets, or Facebook posts with all the information you will cull from here: https://www.fhwa.dot.gov/infrastructure/numbers.cfm.

For those of us in business, reward your customers and clients with their own special highway number with a special surprise note or offer just for them. Consider what services or products they have purchased from you and what you can do or offer to compliment those services. Then gift them with a sample of something new to try or a discount on those products or services. This 'taste test' is often used by food services and beauty product industries. Why not give it a try today? Look in the appendix for a sample Highway Numbers Day Card to get you started. There you will find both the Standard Interstate sign and Business Loop for use in your promotions.

Who am I?

Mar 8 Discover What Your Name Means Day — Today we trace our history, well sort of. It's about making sure your name is a respected, celebrated part of your personhood. Getting together with your clients, customers, or family to discuss the meanings of our names could make for an interesting and fun event. If you don't know the meaning of your name there's a terrific resource in the appendix to help you along the way, but you might also ask your parents or other family members why your unique name was chosen for you when you were born.

Alternatively, why not for your most important clients, create cards that explains what their unique name means? If you are a crafty sort you could design a really special card with their name and meaning on the front and your message in the middle. Small envelopes to fit your design can easily be made, too. See the appendix for a sample and envelope instructions.

You might find a bit of extra fun if you include learning your names in Morse Code or sign language. You can also extend the events around this day for a whole week as today happens to fall in the middle of International Celebrate Your Name Week (Mar 5-11).

Mar 18 Play the Recorder Day — Yes, there really is an American Recorder Society (ARS) and no, it isn't an electrical piece of equipment. Many ARS chapters, consorts, and recorder orchestras plan special concerts and presentations to illustrate the versatility and beauty of this wonderful instrument. Recorders date back to the 14th century. So, have some fun. Strike up the band. Invite your friends and neighbors, clients and customers to join in the fun. Music Teachers, Classroom Teachers, Parent Teachers, and Student Teachers can all use this holiday to share the joy of music with others.

There's always cards and emails, as well as social media that you could share to celebrate, if you don't happen to have the clients and / or talent to celebrate with music.

Mar 21 Twitter Day — Talking about social media, Twitter Day is the perfect day to tweet your heart out! Share posts, create your own hashtag, or use one that is already hotly used. Be sure to increase your re-tweets too. If you are Twitter savvy why not give a course on Twitter etiquette, or maybe how to increase your Twitter or other social media following? Would your customers and clients welcome a Twitter Hashtag Guide? You can use the one I have created and share in the appendix or create your own. Be sure to brand it with your own Brand Identity. And check out the Resources for the link to a helpful hashtag search tool.

Mar 27 Quirky Country Music Song Titles Day — Yes, there are some mighty strange Country Music Song Titles out there. And, today is the day to celebrate them. Here are two to show you what I mean. "I Still Miss You Baby, But My Aim's Gettin' Better" or "You're the main reason Our Youngsters Are Extremely Ugly".

So, to make this a business building day start with contests like "Name that Tune". Never hold up the fun, give prizes and surprises for the winners. You will find a short list of Quirky Country Music Song Titles and their artist in the Appendix. Don't forget to use social media to make your event extra fun.

Mar 31 International Hug a Medievalist Day — Here's a Weird & Wacky Holiday you can wrap your arms around. To celebrate you could interview an author who writes in this genre or have a photo contest on Facebook or your own website. Virtual hugs are allowed. Be sure to check out the approved hugging technique for your safe and legal hugging in the appendix.

APRIL

MONTH-LONG HOLIDAYS

Apr 2 – 15 Passiontide

Alcohol Awareness Month, Black Women's History Month, Community Spirit Days, Defeat Diabetes Month, Distracted Driving Awareness Month, Grange Month, Holy Humor Month, Informed Women Month, International Customer Loyalty Month, International Twit Award Month, Jazz Appreciation Month, Library Snapshot Days, Mathematics Awareness Month, Month of the Young Child®, National African-American Women's Fitness Month, National Autism Awareness Month, National Cancer Control Month, National Card and Letter Writing Month, National Child Abuse Prevention Month, National Decorating Month, National Donate Life Month, National Exchange Club Child Abuse Prevention Month, National Humor Month, National Lawn Care Month, National Occupational Therapy Month, National Pecan Month, National Pest Management Month, National Poetry Month, National Sexual Assault Awareness Month, Nationally Sexually Transmitted Diseases (STDs) Month, National Soy Foods Month, National Youth Sports Safety Month, Pet First Aid Awareness Month, Pharmacists War on Diabetes Month, Prevention of Animal Cruelty Month, Rosacea Awareness Month, School Library Month, Straw Hat Month, Stress Awareness Month, Women's Eye Health & Safety Month, Workplace Conflict Awareness Month, World Landscape Architecture Month, Worldwide Bereaved Spouses Awareness Month

WEEK-LONG HOLIDAYS

Apr 1 – 7 APAWS International Pooper-scooper Week, Laugh at Work Week, Testicular Cancer Awareness Week (aka Get A Grip Day)

Apr 2 – 8 Consider Christianity Week, Greece: Dumb Week, National Crime Victims' Rights Week, National Window Safety Week, Passion Week

Apr 3 – 6 Italy: Bologna Children's Book Fair

Apr 3 – 7 Undergraduate Research Week

Apr 3 – 10 Explore Your Career Options Week

Apr 4 – 10 Hate Week–"Down with Big Brother"

Apr 9 – 15 Orthodox Holy Week, National Library Week, Pan–American Week

Apr 15 – 23 National Park Week

Apr 16 – 22 National Coin Week, National Karaoke Week

Apr 20 – 23 Fiddler's Frolics

Apr 22 – 23 Just Pray No! Worldwide Weekend of Prayer and Fasting

Apr 22 – 29 Money Smart Week®

Apr 23 – 29 Administrative Professionals Week, National Volunteer Week, Preservation Week, Sky Awareness Week

Apr 21 – 28 National Playground Safety Week

Apr 24 – 28 Week of the Young Child

Apr 24 – 30 World Immunization Week

Apr 26 – 29 AQS Quilt Week–Paducah

Apr 28 – 30 National Dream Hotline® Days

Apr 29 – May 5 Japan: Golden Week Days

DAILY HOLIDAYS

1. *April Fool's or All Fool's Day, Canada: Nunavut Independence Day, International Pillow Fight Day, Mylesday, National Love Your Children Day, Reading is Funny Day, *Sorry Charlie Day, US Air force Academy Day

2. Hans Christian Anderson Day (1805), *International Children's Book Day, *Sir Alec Guinness (1914), National Ferret Day, National Love Your Produce Manager Day, Ponce de Leon Discovers Florida (1513), *Reconciliation Day, *United Nations: World Autism Awareness Day, US Mint Day

3. Blacks Ruled Eligible to Vote Day (1944), *Pony Express Day, National Weed Out Hate: Sow the Seeds of Peace Day, Pascua Florida Day (Observed), *Tweed Day

4. *Beatles Take Over Music Charts (50th Anniversary), *Bonza Bottler Day™, Flag Act of 1818 Day, Senegal: Independence Day, Taiwan: Children's Day, *United Nations: International Day for Mine Awareness & Assistance in Mine Action, *Vitamin C Day

5. *Helen Keller's Miracle Day, National Deep Dish Pizza Day, Paraprofessional Appreciation Day

6. Drowsy Driver Awareness Day, National Alcohol Screening Day, National Fun at Work Day, North Pole Discovery Day, *Tartan Day, *Teflon Day (1938), Thailand: Chakri Day, United Nations: International Day of Sport for Development and Peace

7. Education and Sharing Day, *International Beaver Day, International Snailpapers Day, *Metric System Day, National Beer Day (1933), *No Housework Day, United Nations: International Day of the Reflection on the Genocide in Rwanda, *United Nations: World Health Day

8. Home Run Record Set by Hank Aaron (1974), International Roma Day, Japan: Flower Festival (Hana Matsuri), Lazarus Saturday, National Dog Fighting Awareness Day

9. *Civil Rights Bill of 1866 Day, Civil War Ends (1865), *Jenkins Ear Day, Jumbo the Elephant Day, National Former Prisoner of War Recognition Day, Palm Sunday, *Winston Churchill Day

10. ASPCA Incorporation Day (1866), *Commodore Perry Day, *National Siblings Day, Passover begins at Sundown, *Safety Pin Day, *Salvation Army Founder's Day

11. *Barbershop Quartet Day, Children's Day in Florida (always the second Tuesday), International Be Kind to Lawyers Day, *International "Louie Louie" Day, National Equal Pay Day, National Library Workers Day, Pesach or Passover

12. Halifax: Independence Day, National Bookmobile Day, *National D.E.A.R. Day (aka Drop Everything and Read), *National Licorice Day, Polio Vaccine Day, United Nations: International Day of Human Space Flight, *Walk on Your Wild Side Day

13. *Guy Fawkes Day, Maundy Thursday or Holy Thursday, *Thomas Jefferson Day

14. Bermuda: Good Friday Kite Flying Day, *Children with Alopecia Day, Good Friday, India: Vaisakhi, *International Moment of Laughter Day, Pan American Day, Pan–American Day in Florida, Pathologists' Assistant Day

15. Boston Marathon Bombing (2013), Botox Day, Easter Even, *Deaf School Day, *McDonald's Day, *Income Tax Pay Day—But Not this Year, National Auctioneers Day, *National Take a Wild Guess Day, *National That Sucks Day, Record Store Day, *Titanic Sinking (1912)

16. *Charlie Chaplin Day (1889), Easter Sunday, Emancipation Day

17. American Samoa: Flag Day, *Blah! Blah! Blah! Day, Dyngus Day, Easter Monday, *Ellis Island Family History Day, *Income Tax Pay Day—This is Really It, Quarterly Estimated Federal Income Tax Payers' Due Date (also Jan 15, Jun 15, and Sep 15, 2015), International Haiku Poetry Day, South Africa: Family Day, Syrian Arab Republic: Independence Day

18. The House that Ruth Built Day, *International Amateur Radio Day, Stress Awareness Day, Paul Revere's Ride Day (1775), *Pet Owners Independence Day, Third World Day, Zimbabwe: Independence Day

19. Branch Davidian Fire at Waco (1993), John Parker Day, National Hanging Out Day, Oklahoma City Bombing (1995), Patriots Day in Florida

20. National High Five Day, Get to Know Your Customers Day (third Thursday of each quarter is set aside to get to know your customers even better)

21. Aggie Muster Day, Brazil: Tiradentes Day, *Kindergarten Day, National Bulldogs are Beautiful Day, San Jacinto Day

22. Brazil Day, *Chemists Celebrate the Earth Day, Coins Stamped "In God We Trust" Day, *Earth Day, International Home Furnishings Market Day, National Dance Day, *National Jelly Bean Day, Oklahoma Land Rush Day (1889), United Nations: International Mother Earth Day

23. Canada: Newfoundland: Saint George's Day, *Movie Theatre Day, *Public School Day, National English Muffin Day, Spain: Book Day and Lover's Day, Saint George Feast Day, William Shakespeare Day (1564), United Nations: English Language Day, *United Nations: World Book & Copyright Day, World Book Night

24. *Confederate Memorial Day, Ireland: Easter Rising (1916), Library of Congress Day, Mother-Father Deaf Day

25. Abortion Legalized (1967), Anzac Day, Egypt: Sinai Day, *License Plates Day, Swaziland: National Flag Day, World Malaria Day, World Penguin Day

26. Administrative Professionals Day or Secretary's Day, Florida & Georgia: Confederate Memorial Day, *Hug An Australian Day, National Help a Horse Day, National Pretzel Day, *Richter Scale Day, United Nations: World Intellectual Property Day

27. *Babe Ruth Day (1947), Mantanzas Mule Day, *Morse Code Day, Most Tornadoes in a Day (US), National Little Pampered Dog Day, Sierra Leon: Independence Day, Take Our Daughters and Sons to Work® Day (fourth Thursday in April), Togo: Independence Day

28. Arizona: Arbor Day, Biological Clock Gene Discovered (1994), Canada: National Day of Mourning, National Arbor Day, National Hairball Awareness Day, National Teach Children to Save Day, United Nations: World Day for Safety and Health at Work, Workers Memorial Day

29. Japan: Showa Day, National Rebuilding Day, *Peace' Rose Day, Spring Astronomy Day, United Nations: Day of Remembrance for all Victims of Chemical Warfare, World Healing Day, World Tai Chi and Qigong Day, World Veterinary Day, Zipper Day (1913)

30. Beltane, *Bugs Bunny Day (1938), Día de los Niños/Día de los Libros, International Jazz Day, National Animal Advocacy Day, National Honesty Day (Honest Abe Awards), *Spank Out Day USA, Vietnam: Liberation Day, *Walpurgis Night

HOLIDAY MARKETING IDEAS FOR APRIL

Apr 1 – 7 Laugh at Work Week — For one week each year the world celebrates Laugh at Work Week - a week dedicated to having fun at work and recognizing the business value of humor and laughter. Appropriately, the week begins on April 1. That's right, April Fool's Day, the day in which pranks, stunts, practical jokes, and spoofs abound.

Laughter and humor are an important part of the workplace. Benefits of laughing at work include improved *productivity, creativity, teamwork, communication, stress relief, job satisfaction*, and *employee retention*. So, to celebrate have an office party. Enjoy a few giggles on-line or off-line, whatever the case may be for you and your team. Lighten things up a bit, take the time to share funny stories while getting to know your customers and/or staff. A simple fun card is a good start, but a party is so much more fun!

One way to celebrate is to have a photo caption contest. Have contestants share a fun photo or post a few to choose from and ask for captions. The frivolity will abound, and you might just make a new friend or two. If you are a writer, editor, publisher, you might start a humorous story and have others add a line or paragraph. Those types of activities are sure to put a smile on all participants' faces.

If your business caters to any of the previously mentioned benefits of laughter in the workplace, then you have every excuse to have an event and share your expertise. And, you have a whole week to do it!

Apr 2 National Ferret Day — Did you know that male ferrets are called Hobs and female ferrets are called Jills? Their offspring are called Kits. The whole family is called a Business. So make it your Business to ferret out the animal lover in all of those you come in contact with today. I know that was pretty bad, even for me.

Share some ferret facts. Give them out on cards that you have branded, post them on social media. Pinterest would make a terrific place to start your fun facts about ferret's day! You'll find a card I created to spark your creative juices in the appendix.

Apr 7 International Beaver Day — It sure seems like the animals have taken over this month! Here we go with one more for your marketing pleasure. Beavers are known for the dams they build. Stopping up rivers and streams and causing mischief and mayhem in the process. With that thought in mind think of ways you can help others tear down the dams in their lives, and the lives of their businesses. Instead of gnawing on trees, try chewing on ideas to create unstoppable results in your business because you and your customers and clients are "Worth a Dam!" Sorry, I couldn't help myself.

Busy beaver that you are, take the time to step aside for your health and shower your customers and friends with relaxing activities and products. If you sell relaxation products, are a meditation coach, or serve the community in any other

Photograph by Steve Hersey

capacity that involves health or stress relief products, holding an event to showcase those products and services is another fine way to market your business on International Beaver Day!

However, if you work with children, both young and old, one fun activity you could have is pin the tail on the beaver. You'll find the pieces you need in the appendix. I have designed it in vector so if you need a larger image for your Weird & Wacky holiday event, contact me and I'll make sure you have what you need to ensure your party animal is taken care of on International Beaver Day.

Apr 12 National Licorice Day — According to Licorice International, this sweet treat has been around for a very, very long time. They state it is rife with health benefits, everything from the common cough to high blood pressure and its related complications. So, to celebrate National Licorice Day, think about health services.

It could be the health of your business as well as the health of your body you can celebrate with events, cards, and even just buying a box to hand out with your business card or flier.

If you know a physical trainer or physician, so much the better. Work with them to hold an event to share tips and tricks to improve your attendees. But, as I mentioned before, it could be your focus will be the health of your customers and their businesses, rather than your physical being. Either way, be sure to take advantage of this opportunity to get your name out there. Why not build your reputation for being the fun and savvy go-to person in your niche?

Apr 18 Third World Day — Here in America we take so much for granted. But, in other places the simple things like clean water and shelter, and the basic necessities are often a luxury. Even a pair of shoes, for some, could be a true gift. So, today I suggest you volunteer at a homeless shelter, if you want to make a real impact. Or you might consider a charity drive. This could be for shoes or other basic necessities; it doesn't have to be just about raising money. It could be about raising awareness.

In my church we have an annual project called 'Drop Your Drawers'. We donate underwear, socks, and the like that are given to school aged children who otherwise would go without through Clothes to Kids. Yes, right here is the good ol' USA kids of all ages go without these basic necessities.

If you choose to have a fund raiser of any sort, be sure to let the media know what you are up to. They just love a break from all the negative news! And, so do we.

Apr 23 Muffin Day — Who doesn't love muffins!? Considering all the scrumptious flavors to try this holiday could be a tasty new tradition for your business or your family. I suggest you use the card that I designed, which you will find in the appendix. On the back of it, write a favorite muffin recipe to ensure the recipient will retain it and perhaps even put it on their coveted refrigerator space. You'll find eleven delectable muffin recipes in the appendix courtesy of Bustle.com.

MAY

MONTH-LONG HOLIDAYS

May 29 – Jun 4 Black Single Parent's Week

Asian/Pacific American Heritage Month, Asthma Awareness Month, Better Hearing and Speech Month, Fibromyalgia Education and Awareness Month, Gardening for Wildlife Month, Get Caught Reading Month, Gifts from the Garden Month, Global Civility Awareness Month, Haitian Heritage Month, Healthy Vision Month, Huntington's Disease Awareness Month, International Mediterranean Diet Month, International Victorious Woman Month, Jewish American Heritage Month, Melanoma/Skin Cancer Detection and Prevention Month, Mental Health Month, Motorcycle Safety Month, Mystery Month, National Allergy/Asthma Awareness Month, National Arthritis Awareness Month, National Barbecue Month, National Bike Month, National Foster Care Month, National Good Car-Keeping Month, National Hamburger Month, National Hepatitis Awareness Month, National Meditation Month, National Military Appreciation Month, National Osteoporosis Awareness and Prevention Month, National Photo Month, National Physical Fitness and Sports Month, National Preservation Month, National Salad Month, National Stroke Awareness Month, National Sweet Vidalia® Onion Month, National Vinegar Month, Older American's Month, React Month, Spiritual Literacy Month, Strike Out Strokes Month, Ultraviolet Awareness Month, Women's Health Care Month, Worldwide Home Schooling Awareness Month, Young Achievers/Leaders of Tomorrow Month

WEEK-LONG HOLIDAYS

May 1 – 7 Children's Book Week, Choose Privacy Week, National Wildflower Week

May 1 – 5 PTA Teacher Appreciation Week

May 6 – 12 National Nurses Week

May 7 – 13 Be Kind to Animals Week®, Goodwill Industries Week, National Family Week, National Hug Holiday Week, National Pet Week, Root Canal Awareness Week, Update Your References Week

May 8 – 12 National Etiquette Week

May 8 – 14 National Stuttering Awareness Week

May 14 – 20 National Police Week, National Transportation Week, Salute to 35+ Moms Week, Work at Home Moms Week

May 16 – 21 National Foul Ball Week

May 19 – 21 Fishing Has No Boundaries Days

May 20 – 26 National Safe Boating Week

May 21 – 27 International New Friends Old Friends Week, National Hurricane Preparedness Week, World Trade Week

May 22 – 29 National Backyard Games Week

May 24 – 30 Fleet Week New York 2017

May 31 – Jun 1 Shavuot

May 31 – Jun 2 Book Expo America Trad Exhibit (Javits Center NY, NY)

DAILY HOLIDAYS

1. *Amtrak, Great Britain Formed Day (1707), *Keep Kids Alive — Drive 25° Day, Labor Day, *Law Day, *Lei Day, *Loyalty Day, *May Day, Melanoma Monday, Mother Goose Day, National Bubba Day, *New Home Owners Day, *School Principals' Day

2. Double No-Hitter Day (1917), Israel: Independence Day, King James Bible Day, National Teachers Day, World Asthma Day

3. Dow Jones Tops 11,000 Day (1999), *Garden Meditation Day, James Brown (1993), Japan: Constitution Memorial Day, *Lumpy Rug Day, Mexico: Day of the Holy Cross, National Public Radio Day, National Specially-Abled Pets Day, *National Two Different Colored Shoes Day, *United Nations: World Press Freedom Day

4. China: Youth Day, Curaçao: Memorial Day, Jamaica Discover Day (1494), *International Respect for Chickens Day, Japan: Greenery Day, National Day of Prayer, National Day of Reason, *Star Wars Day

5. AMA Founded Day (1847), *Bonza Bottler Day™, *Cartoonists' Day, *Cinco de Mayo, International Day of the Midwife, Japan: Children's Day, South Korea: Children's Day, Thailand: Coronation Day

6. Free Comic Book Day, *Joseph Brackett Day, Kentucky Derby, Martin Z Mollusk Day, *No Diet Day, *No Homework Day, Orson Wells Day (1915)

7. Beaufort Scale Day, Dow Jones Tops 15000 (2013), Motorcycle Mass and Blessing of the Bikes, National Cosmopolitan Day, National Infertility Survival® Day

8. *No Socks Day, *United Nations: Time of Remembrance & Reconciliation WWII (8 – 9), *V E Day, *World Red Cross Red Crescent Day

9. European Union Founded (1950)

10. Donate A Day's Wages To Charity Day, Golden Spike Driving Day, National Bike to School Day, National Nightshift/Thirdshift Workers Day, National Receptionists Day, National School Nurse Day, Singapore: Day of Vesak, World Lupus Day

11. *Eat What You Want Day, Military Spouse Appreciation Day

12. Fintastic Friday: Giving Sharks a Voice Day, *Limerick Day, Military Spouse Appreciation Day, Native American Rights Day (1879), *Odometer Day

13. Children of Fallen Patriots Day, International Migratory Bird Celebration (Day), Jamestown Day, Letter Carriers "Stamp Out Hunger" Food Drive, *Jamestown Day, National Hummus Day, Stay Up All Night Night, United Nations: World Migratory Bird Day, World Fair Trade Day

14. Lag B'Omer, *Lewis and Clark Expedition Sets Out Day (1804), Mother's Day, Mother's Day at the Wall, Smallpox Vaccine Discovery (1796), Spring Astronomy Day,*The Stars and Stripes Forever Day, *Underground America Day, WAAC Day (1942)

15. Flight Attendant Day, Hyperemesis Gravidarum Awareness Day, Japan: Aoi Matsuri (Hollyhock Festival), Mexico: San Isidro Day, National Sliders Day, *Nylon Stockings Day, *Peace Officer Memorial Day, *United Nations: International Day of Families

16. *Academy Awards Day (1929), *Biographer's Day, *First Woman to Climb Mt Everest Day (1975), Mimosa Day

17. *First Kentucky Derby Day (1875), *Same-Sex Marriages Day (2004), *United Nations: World Telecommunications and Information Society Day

18. Haiti: Flag and University Day, *International Museum Day, *Visit Your Relatives Day

19. *Boys Club Day, Endangered Species Day, International Virtual Assistants Day, National Bike to Work Day, *National Defense Transportation Day, National Hepatitis Testing Day, *National Pizza Party Day, National Scooter Day, Teacher's Day in Florida

20. *Amelia Earhart Atlantic Crossing Day (1932), Armed Forces Day, *Eliza Doolittle Day, Lindbergh Flight (1927), Mecklenburg Day, National Learn to Swim Day, *Weights & Measures Day

21. *American Red Cross Founder's Day, *I Need A Patch For That Day, *National Wait Staff Day, Neighbor Day, Rogation Sunday, Rural Life Sunday or Soil Stewardship Sunday, *United Nations: World Day for Cultural Diversity for Dialogue & Development

22. Canada: Victoria Day, *Canadian Immigrants' Day, Mr. Rogers Neighborhood Day, *National Maritime Day, Strongest Earthquake in the 20th Century (1960), *United Nations: International Day for Biological Diversity, World Goth Day

23. *Bonnie and Clyde Death (1934), *Declaration of the Bab Day, *International World Turtle Day®, United Nations: International day to End Obstetric Fistula

24. *Brother's Day, Eritrea: Independence Day, International Tiara Day, Israel: Yom Yerushalayim, *Morse Code Day

25. African Freedom Day, Ascension Day, *Ralph Waldo Emerson (1803), *Jessie Owens' Day, Jordan: Independence Day, Memory Days, National Eat More Fruits and Vegetables Day, *National Missing Children's Day, *National Tap Dance Day, Poetry Day in Florida, *Towel Day, United Nations: Week of Solidarity with Peoples of Non-Self-Governing Territories

26. Australia: Sorry Day, John Wayne (1907), World Lindy Hop Day

27. *Cellophane Tape Day, *Golden Gate Bridge Day, Julia Pierpoint Day, Ramadan

28. *Amnesty International Founded (1961), Haiti: Mother's Day, Indianapolis 500, *Sierra Club Day, *Slugs Return From Capistrano Day

29. *Amnesty for Southern Rebels Day, Memorial Day, *Mount Everest Summit Reached (1953), *Memorial Day (Traditional), Prayer for Peace, *United Nations: International Day of United Nations Peacekeepers

30. *First American Daily Newspaper Published (1783), *Indianapolis 500 Anniversary (1911), *Loomis Day, Memorial Day (Traditional), Saint Joan of Arc Feast Day, Shavuot (begins at sundown), *World Trade Center Recovery and Cleanup Ends (2002)

31. *Copyright Law Passed (1970), National Senior Health and Fitness Day, Shavuot, *United Nations: World No–Tobacco Day, *What You Think Upon Grows Day, *Walt Whitman Day

HOLIDAY MARKETING IDEAS FOR MAY

Better Hearing and Speech Month— It's time for all to improve our communications skills. Offering training or testing clinics in these areas are the immediate thoughts that come to mind. However, if you aren't career focused on these types of professions you, too, can participate in organizing or hosting your event. Sponsoring one would be the easiest way, but hands on is much more satisfying. ASHA has a great 'kit' just waiting for you to use. You'll find their link in the appendix.

Other things you might consider to promote your business throughout the month of May could include social media posts and photos, email campaigns, blog tours, and even the simple card. After all, a card is just the written word.

IDENTIFY THE **SIGNS**

Also, you might consider reading a book to a group of children, or if you are an author, why not schedule a reading at your local library? Keep your thinking cap on and I am sure you'll come up with some outstanding ideas to celebrate the month of May!

May 14–20 Salute to 35+ Moms Week & Work at Home Moms Week—This is your chance to host a business summit for women and moms who are either working at home or want to. So many topics could be addressed that I am sure you will find plenty of speakers to fill the time. Keep the tickets reasonably priced and consider holding a contest for two free tickets. This will help you promote your event as you seek sponsors and speakers. You will find a handout you can brand to your own company in the appendix.

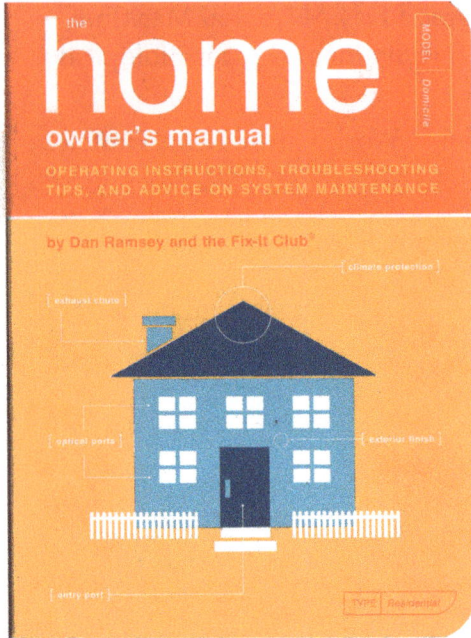

May 1 New Home Owners Day—Whether this is you (think house-warming party) or your niche, you have a whole plethora of ideas you could implement to share your business. Everything from finding out who are new home owners in your neighborhood and making the rounds to introduce yourself with a bag of cookies (with your business coupon or card attached for sure) to New Home Owner Tips, tweets, social media shares, and even events. All these ways and more could ingratiate you to the new folks in your local area.

Why not consider partnering with a business in your area and giving out a coupon from them as you make your rounds. With all the dough they spent to get their new home, the packing, and unpacking, I bet they would be much appreciative of pizza from the neighborhood pizza joint or a nice relaxing spa coupon from a salon near them.

If you are worried about the cost of purchasing a list, I've got you covered. Check out the appendix for a website called Welcome Card where you can find the information you seek for as little as 20¢ per name.

May 10 National Nightshift/Thirdshift Workers Day—If you've always wanted to try staying u know some teens who do, this could be your golden opportunity. Consider this idea. Partner with a florist. Yes, they will donate or discount for special opportunities to promote their business. They donate flowers and you and your 'team' visit a business that employs third shift workers. Businesses that come immediately to mind are hospital workers and emergency services, e.g., firemen.

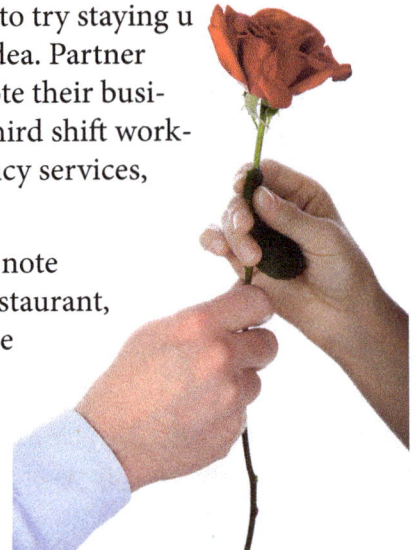

Hand out one flower to each worker with the flower shop card and your branded note attached with a pretty little ribbon. You might even find a third business, like a restaurant, who might wants to get in on the fun. Be sure to send out a press release to tell the media what you and your florist of choice are up to.

May 12 Odometer Day—For starters to celebrate this Weird & Wacky holiday use #NationalOdometerDay to post on social media. Your odometer measures the distance you have traveled. So, when I think about what can be done to celebrate the answer is simple, find ways to help others increase their business

successes. If you have an SEO company, or are a business coach this should be a no-brainer. Feel free to use the Odometer card in the appendix that has been designed with this holiday in mind.

Whatever you do, make sure you measure your marketing success to ensure you, too, are staying on the road to success.

May 21 I Need a Patch for That Day—Today we celebrate anything to do with patches. From coders to seamstresses, there's a patch for most everything. Are you a handyman/woman? Is it time to fix that furniture or learn how? Talk about learning how, there's an idea that you can fix your mind on.

Helping your customers and clients in problem areas they have in their businesses and lives might just be the tool you need. Think teleseminar, webinar, seminar, Google hangouts, and the like.

Maybe you only have time for tweets or social media posts. Here's a fun idea. Have folks submit 'patch designs' or create patches for them. Then, post them on Pinterest or other social media sites. Here's a few to get your synapses sparking: Allergy Patch; Ace That Test; Fill My Bank Account; Willpower; Better Diet; Computer Malfunction. And the list goes on! I designed this one myself. I bet you will come up with some even better ideas.

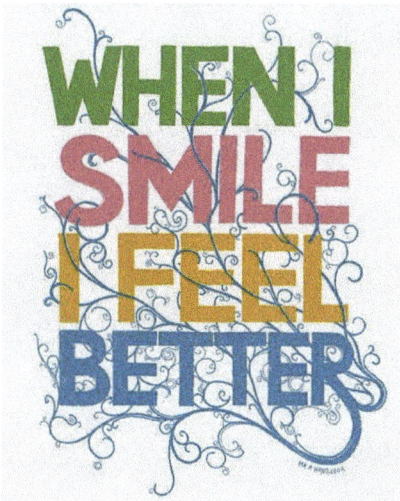

May 31 What You Think Upon Grows Day—The timeless wisdom of Norman Vincent Peale's *Think and Grow Rich;* James Allen quote, "All that man achieves and all that he fails to achieve is the direct result of his own thoughts,"; and the Holy Bible's verse, "If anything is excellent or praiseworthy, think about such things" (Philippians 4:8, TNIV), all remind us of the importance of keeping our minds filled with positive thoughts and ideas. So today, help others today remember that to change their thoughts will change their lives.

While we all know you can't think yourself to success, exactly, your thoughts do have an impact on your health and your life. Therefore, your thoughts are just the beginning. Positive quotes posted on social media, tips, mental and meditation training and events, cards and notes, all of these are great ideas to showcase your business on this very important Weird & Wacky holiday!

JUNE

MONTH-LONG HOLIDAYS

Jun 1 – Nov 27 Afterward — A Special Exhibition

Adopt A Shelter Cat Month, African–American Music Appreciation Month, Audiobook Appreciation Month, Cancer From the Sun Month, Caribbean–American Heritage Month, Cataract Awareness Month, Child Vision Awareness Month, Dairy Alternative Month, Dementia Care Professionals Month, Effective Communications Month, Entrepreneurs & Do It Yourself Marketing Month, Fireworks Safety Month, Gay & Lesbian Pride Month, Great Outdoors Month, International Men's Month, International Surf Music Month, June Dairy Month, Perennial Gardening Month, GLBT (Gay, Lesbian, Bisexual & Transgender) Pride Month, Men's Health Education and Awareness Month, Migraine Awareness Month, National Aphasia Awareness Month, National Bathroom Reading Month, National Candy Month, National Caribbean–American Heritage Month, National GLBT Book Month, National Iced Tea Month, National Oceans Month, National Rivers Month, Nation Safety Month, National Soul Food Month, National Zoo and Aquarium Month, Pharmacists Declare War on Alcoholism Month, PTSD Awareness Month, Skyscraper Month, Student Safety Month

WEEK-LONG HOLIDAYS

Jun 3 – 4 Bookcon 2017 (Javits Center, NY, NY)

Jun 3 – 10 International Clothesline Week

Jun 4 – 10 Bed Bug Awareness Week, National Business Etiquette Week

Jun 11 – 17 National Flag Week

Jun 13 – 20 National Hermit Week

Jun 15 – 22 National Nursing Assistants Week

Jun 16 – 17 Czech Days

Jun 18 – 24 Carpenter Ant Awareness Week, Lightning Safety Awareness Week, Meet a Mate Week

Jun 22 – 25 Little Bighorn Days

Jun 22 – 27 American Library Association Annual Conference (Chicago, IL)

Jun 23 – 25 Coin, Jewelry, & Stamp Expo (Elks Lodge, Pasadena, CA), Colorado Brewers' Festival (Ft. Collins, CO)

Jun 24 – 25 ARRL Field Day

Jun 25 – Jul 1 Windjammer Days

Jun 29 – Jul 24 Freedom Days

DAILY HOLIDAYS

1. China: International Children's Day, *Heimlich Maneuver Day, Say Something Nice Day, Superman Day, United Nations: Global Day of Parents
2. Bahamas: Labor Day, Hug Your Cat Day, Italy: Republic Day, Marquis de Sade Birth (1740), National Donut Day, National Gun Violence Awareness Day, Saint Erasmus Day, United Kingdom: Coronation Day, *Yell Fudge at the Cobras in North America Day (Don't laugh, I haven't seen any lately!)
3. *Chimborazo Day, Confederate Memorial Day, *First Woman Rabbi (1972), *Mighty Casey Struck Out Day (1888), National Trails Day, Zoot Suit Riots Anniversary (1943)
4. China: Tienanmen Square Massacre (1989), Finland: Flag Day, Japan: Day of the Rice God, National Cancer Survivors Day, Orthodox Pentecost, Pulitzer Prize Day (1917), *United Nations: International Day of Innocent Children Victims of Aggression Day, Whitsunday
5. *AIDS First Noted (1981), *Apple II (1977), Baby Boomers Recognition Day, *Hot Air Balloon Day (1783), *United Nations: World Environment Day
6. *Bonza Bottler Day™, *D–Day (1944), *Drive in Movie Day (1933), Germany: Waldchestag (Forest Day), Korea: Memorial Day, National Yo-yo Day, Prop 13 (1978), *SEC Day (1934), Sweden: National Day
7. *(Daniel) Boone Day, Malta: National Day, National Running Day, Supreme Court Strikes Down Connecticut Law Banning Contraception (1965)
8. First Heroine Woman Rewarded (1697), National Caribbean-American HIV/AIDS Awareness Day, *United Nations: World Ocean Day, *Upsy Daisy Day, World Oceans Day
9. *Donald Duck Day, International Archives Day
10. *AA Day (1935), American Mint Day (1652), *Ball Point Pen Day (1943), Belmont Stakes, National Marina Day (tentative), Day of Portugal
11. Children's Sunday, Jacques Cousteau (1910), *Kamehameha Day (First Hawaiian King), Race Unity Day, Trinity Sunday
12. *Baseball's First Perfect Game (1880), National Jerky Day, Loving v Virginia Day (1967), Orlando Nightclub Massacre (2016), Philippines: Independence Day, Queen's Official Birthday (Selected Nations), Russia: Russia Day, *"Tear Down This Wall" Day, United Nations: World Day Against Child Labor
13. Roller Coaster Day (1884), United Nations: International Albinism Awareness Day
14. Alzheimer Day, *Family History Day, *Flag Day, Japan: Rice Planting Festival, UNIVAC Computer Day, US Army Day, World Blood Donor Day
15. Corpus Christi, *Magna Carta Day (1215), National Nursing Assistants Day, Native American Citizenship Day, *Nature Photography Day, Quarterly Estimated Federal Income Tax Payers' Due Date (also Jan 17, Apr 17, June 15, and Sep 15, 2015), United Nations: World Elder Abuse Awareness Day
16. *Bloomsday, House Divided Speech (1858), *Ladies' Day (Baseball), South Africa: Youth Day, Work@Home Father's Day
17. *Apartheid Day, Bunker Hill Day, Iceland: Independence Day, Longest Dam Race Day, Polar Bear Swim, *United Nations: World Day To Combat Desertification and Drought, World Juggling Day
18. *Battle of Waterloo (1815), Egypt: Evacuation Day, Father's Day, Husband Caregiver Day, Seychelles: Constitution Day, US: Corpus Christi (observed)
19. Belmont Stakes Day, *Garfield the Cat Day (1978), *Juneteenth, Texas: Emancipation Day, United Nations: International Day for the Elimination of Sexual Violence in Conflict, War of 1812, "War is Hell" Day (1879), *World Sauntering Day
20. Argentina: Flag Day, *First Doctor of Science Earned by a Woman Day (1895), *United Nations: World Refugee Day

21. Anne and Samantha Day (also Dec 21), Go Skateboarding Day, Midsummer Day/Eve Celebrations, United Nations: International Day of Yoga, World Humanist Day, World Music Day/Fête de la Musique

22. Malta: Mnarja, Stupid Guy Thing Day, V-for Victory Day, Watermelon Thump and Seed-Spitting Contest Day

23. *Let It Go Day, National Eat at a Food Truck Day, Runner's Selfie Day, Take Your Dog To Work Day®, Typewriter Day, United Nations: International Widows Day, United Nations: Public Service Day

24. Canada: Saint John the Baptist Day, *Celebration of the Senses Day, China: Macau Day, "Flying Saucer" Day, Great American Backyard Campout Day, National Haskap Berry Day, Saint John the Baptist Day

25. Log Cabin Day, Mozambique: Independence Day, Singing on the Mountain Day, Supreme Court Ruling Day (Abortion Notification, Bans School Prayer, Upholds Rights to Die), United Nations: Day of the Seafarer

26. *Barcode Day, Canada: Discover Day (Newfoundland and Labrador), CN Tower Day (1976), Federal Credit Union Act (1934), Human Genome Mapped (2000), Saint Lawrence Seaway Dedication (1959), Supreme Court Strikes Down Defense of Marriage Act (2013), United Nations Charter Signing (1945), *United Nations: International Day Against Drug Abuse and Illicit Trafficking, *United Nations: International Day in Support of Victims of Torture

27. *Decide To Be Married Day, *Happy Birthday to "Happy Birthday To You" Day, Industrial Workers of the World Day, National Columnist's Day, *National HIV Testing Day, PTSD Awareness Day

28. Monday Holiday Law (1968), Treaty of Versailles (1919)

29. *Death Penalty Ban Day, Interstate Highway System Born (1956), National Handshake Day, Saint Peter and Paul Day, Saint Peter's Day, Seychelles: Independence Day

30. Britain Cedes Claim to Hong Kong (1997), Charles Blondin's Conquest of Niagara Falls (1859), Congo: Independence Day, *Leap Second Adjustment Time Day, *NOW (National Organization of Women) Founded Day (1966)

HOLIDAY MARKETING IDEAS FOR JUNE

Skyscraper Month — A developer in China built a complete 57-story skyscraper in just 19 days! Now it's your turn; but unlike China, you have a whole month to build on your business' success. Here's your Skyscraper Challenge! This month focus on reviewing your past successes and failures. Figure out what worked and develop your new business building plan for your successful future.

I am thinking about career coaches, recruiters, and any other training that might help you improve in an area of your life or business life that needs a little boost up the ladder of success. Again, tips, pamphlets, fliers, cards, eCards, social media posts, maybe even an Infographic, if not an event are viable options for you this month. Since you have a whole month, why not try several! Be sure to check out the appendix for a Skyscraper flier to help in promoting your event.

Jun 2 Hug Your Cat Day — Today is a terrific day to spend time sharing cat photos, postings, and such. But, did you know that studies have shown that hugs from animals can lower blood pressure and decrease stress? So, think about other stress related things you can do, or events you could hold to help others with their stress related lives. I found a fun poster on social media that

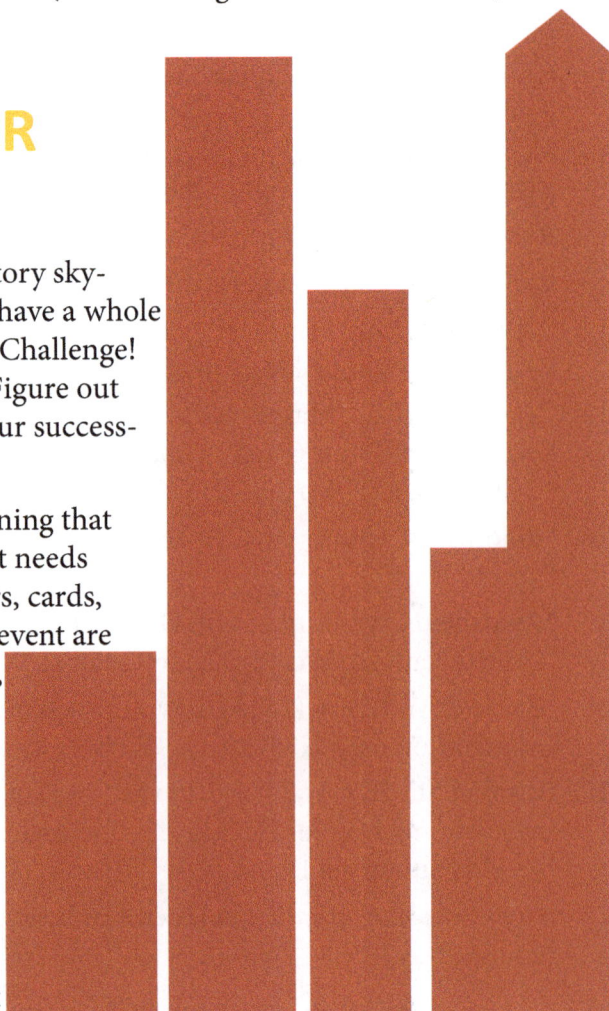

I just have to share, titled, "How to Hug a Cat". I hope you enjoy it, too. You might even be able to come up with an idea of how to incorporate part of it in your business promotion materials for this special day.

Other activities you could participate in are charity fund raisers or donations for your local cat rescue. Cat rescue shelters are always in need of donations, whether in the way of food and litter or monetary donations. You could also join others and volunteer if you have some extra time and love to give. Be sure to let the media know if you plan on doing any of these activities. It's another 'feel good' story for your local media.

Jun 7 National Running Day — Take strides to a healthier lifestyle today. Get a group together and at least walk around the park, or sign up for a charity run. While you are at it, why not schedule a fitness day filled with healthy activities for local residents? Sharing how to make healthier lifestyle choices, and booths with nutrition as a focus would make great displays for your event. Nutritionists, physical trainers, dietitians, doctors, and even music or speaking (think breathing techniques) related fields are types of businesses who will find this an easy day to promote their businesses.

Another fine way to use this Weird & Wacky holiday to promote your business is with a goal- centered business event. Your theme could be "Run to Meet Your Goals", or something similar.

If you aren't into a quick jog around the park, you can always share with photo contests or healthy recipe swaps. Whatever you choose to do, make it fun and it will make it easier for both you and your participants to continue.

Jun 16 Work@Home Father's Day — Father's Day is just around the corner, so I couldn't pass up focusing on the men who often get overlooked when they take on the caregiver roll.

Jeff Zbar is the founder of this Weird & Wacky holiday. You might take his lead and do like he did in 2002, run an essay contest, "Why I Work @ Home: A Father's View." To enter he asked that "Why I Work@Home: A Father's View," entrants must be fathers with at least one in-home, minor child, and must work or telework from a home office at least one day each week. They submitted a 250-word essay on how working from home has improved the balance between their family and professional lives.

I think this is a great way for you to feature this Weird & Wacky holiday and it should be easy enough to find sponsors to donate prizes for the lucky winning Work@Home Dad.

Feel free to use this graphic I designed just for you when making your marketing pieces. You'll find a larger version in the appendix along with a sample essay contest flier.

Jun 21 Go Skateboarding Day — Skateboarding is not just a passing phenomenon. It's definitely here to stay. And, to ensure the longevity of this pastime we now have Go Skateboarding Day. At the official website of International Association of Skateboard Companies (IASC) you can find out all about this Weird & Wacky holiday. And, of course, you'll find the link, as always, in the appendix at the end of this book.

So, to celebrate we turn our attention to fund raisers, demos, contests, and the like. According to Wikipedia: "In 2006, more than 350 events took place in 32 countries around the world." (https://en.wikipedia.org/wiki/Go_Skateboarding_Day)

Businesses the likes of Nike, Samsung, Red Bull, and even the Olympics realize there's something about skateboarding

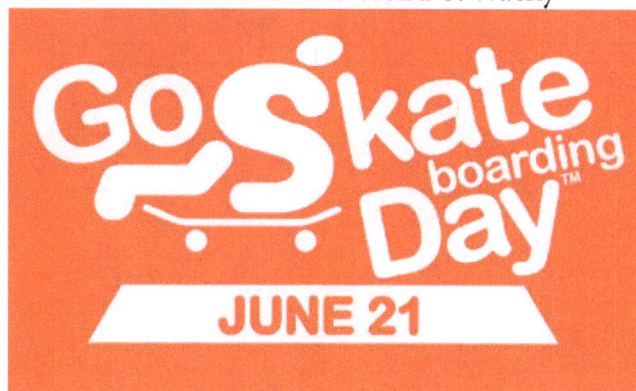

that just works. That's a good reason for you and your business to join in on the festivities. Sponsor, if you can, an event in your local area, or if you are a podcaster or blogger you can always find a skateboarder to share their love for this popular sport.

At the very least you should get on your favorite social media channel and share in the frivolity of this previously thought notorious sport.

Jun 29 **Saint Peter and Paul Day** — In the religious community this is an important day. To take advantage of the saints before you, it helps to know a bit about these two. So, tweets about them and things they did, including how to follow their lead, would be an easy way to start your promotions.

Reading to children, coloring book contests, collages, and anything else arts and crafty are also things that can easily be done by event participants. How about "A Day in the Life of a Saint" for a title to your promo piece or event?

Since 1895, this feast day has acquired a new significance as a commemoration of the "Burning of the Arms", the Doukhobors' destruction of their weapons, as a symbol of their refusal to participate in government-sponsored killing. (https://en.wikipedia.org/wiki/Feast_of_Saints_Peter_and_Paul)

Therefore, alternative events could be focused around peacekeeping or any number of relaxation techniques or business wares.

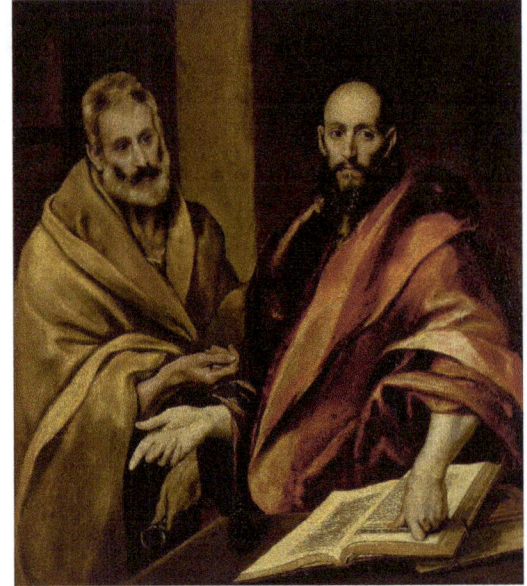

JULY

MONTH-LONG HOLIDAYS

Jul 3 – Aug 11 Dog Days
Jul 3 – Aug 15 Air Conditioning Appreciation Days

Alopecia Month for Women, International, Bioterrorism/Disaster Education & Awareness Month, Cell Phone Courtesy Month, Get Ready for Kindergarten Month, Herbal/Prescription Awareness Month, International Zine Month, National "Doghouse Repairs" Month, National Grilling Month, National Horseradish Month, National Hot Dog Month, National Ice Cream Month, National Make a Difference to Children Month, National Minority Mental Health Awareness Month, National Recreation & Parks Month, National Vacation Rental Month, National Watermelon Month, Smart Irrigation Month, Women's Motorcycle Month, Worldwide Bereaved Parents Awareness Month

WEEK-LONG HOLIDAYS

Jul 1 – 4 National Tom Sawyer Days

Jul 2 – 8 Be Nice to Jersey Week

Jul 7 – 14 Spain: Running of the Bulls

Jul 9 – 15 National Farrier's Week, Sports Cliché Week

Jul 10 – 16 Nude Recreation Week

Jul 16 – 22 Captive Nations Week

Jul 18 – 25 Restless Leg Syndrome (RLS) Education and Awareness Week

Jul 20 – 23 Comic–Con International, Hemingway Look–alike Contest

Jul 22 – 30 National Moth Week

Jul 26 – 30 Oregon Brewers Festival

Jul 26 – Aug 6 Ohio State Fair

Jul 28 – 30 Annie Oakley Days, Compassionate Friends National Conference (Orlando, FL), Lollapalooza

Jul 28 – Aug 5 Montana State Fair

Jul 29 – Aug 5 England: Cowes Week

Jul 30 – Aug 5 Single Working Women's Week

Jul 31 – Aug 1 Moby Dick Marathon

DAILY HOLIDAYS

1. Canada: Canada Day, China: Half-year Day, *IRS Day (1862), *Estée Lauder Day (1906), *First Photographs Used in Newspaper Report (1848), *First Scheduled Television Broadcast (1941), Postage Stamp Day, *Second Half of the New Year Day, United Nations: International Day of Cooperatives, *Zip Code Day, Zoo Day

2. Amelia Earhart Disappears (1937), *Civil Rights Day, *Constitution Day (USA), Declaration of Independence Resolution (1776), Ducktona 500, First Solo Round-the-World Balloon Flight (2002), Halfway Point of 2017

3. Air-conditioning Appreciation Days, Belarus: Independence Day, Caribbean Day or Caricom Day, *Compliment Your Mirror Day, *Canada: Québec Founded, *Stay Out Of The Sun Day

4. *Anne Landers (95th Anniversary), Celebration of the Cane Day, Declaration of Independence Signing (1776), *Fourth of July or Independence Day, *Independence-from–Meat Day, *Lou Gehrig Day (1939), Zambia: Unity Day

5. *Bikini Day, *National Labor Relations Day, Venezuela: Independence Day

6. Comoros: Independence Day, First Airship Crossing of the Atlantic (1919), Name That Tune Day, *Rabies Inoculation Day, *Take Your Webmaster to Lunch Day

7. *Bonza Bottler Day™, *Father–Daughter Take a Walk Together Day, Japan: Tanabata (Star Festival), Solomon Islands: Independence Day, Spain: Running of the Bulls, *Tell The Truth Day

8. Aspinwall Crosses US on Horseback (1911), Bald Is In Day, Carver Day, *SCUD Day (Savor the Comic, Unplug the Drama), Stone House Day

9. Argentina: Independence Day, First Open Heart Surgery Day (1893), *Martyrdom of The Bab, South Sudan: Independence Day

10. Bahamas: Independence Day, *Clerihew Day, *Don't Step On A Bee Day, International Town Criers Day

11. Bowdler's Day, *Day of the Five Billion, *United Nations: World Population Day

12. Family Feud Day (1976), Kiribati: Independence Day, Night of Nights, Northern Ireland: Orangemen's Day, São Tomé and Príncipe: Independence Day

13. *Embrace Your Geekness Day, *Gruntled Workers Day, World Cup Day (1930)

14. Children's Party at Green Animals Day, England: Birmingham Riots Day (1791), France: Night Watch (Bastille Day), National Motorcycle Day

15. Canada: *Saint Swithin's Day, Japan: Bon Odori (Feast of Lanterns), National Woodie Wagon Day, *Rembrandt Day, Toss Away the "Could Haves" and "Should Haves" Day

16. Atomic Bomb Test Day, National Ice Cream Day

17. Astor Day, Disneyland Opened (1955), Japan: Marine Day (Third Monday in July), Minimum Legal Drinking Age at 21 Day, National Get Out of the Doghouse Day, Puerto Rico: Muñoz–Rivera Day, "Wrong Way" Corrigan Day (1938)

18. Mandela Day, Red Skelton Day (1913), United Nations: Nelson Mandela International Day

19. *Art Linkletter (1912), Elvis Presley First Single Day, Saint Vincent de Paul Day, Take Your Poet to Work Day

20. Columbia: Independence Day, Get to Know Your Customers Day (third Thursday of each quarter is set aside to get to know your customers even better), Riot Act Day, *Special Olympics Day

21. Belgium: Independence Day, *Hemingway (1899), No Pet Store Puppies Day

22. National Day of the Cowboy, *Pied Piper Day, *Rat-catchers Day, *Spooner's (Spoonerism) Day

23. Auntie's Day, Egypt: Revolution Day, *Hot Enough for Ya Day, Japan: Soma No Umaoi (Wild Horse Chasing)

24. Amelia Earhart Day, *Cousins Day, *National Drive-Thru Day, *National Tell An Old Joke Day, Pioneer Day

25. First Airplane Crossing of English Channel (1909), Spain: Saint James Day, *Test–Tube Baby Day (1978)

26. Americans with Disabilities Day, Armed Forces Unified (1947), Cuba: National Day (1953), Curaçao Day, *Esperanto Book Day, *George Bernard Shaw (1856), Liberia & Maldives: Independence Day, *US Army Desegregation Day (1944)

27. *Atlantic Telegraph Day, *Insulin Isolated Day (1921), *National Korean War Veterans Armistice Day, National Chili Dog Day, *Take Your Houseplant for a Walk Day, *Walk on Stilts Day

28. Beatrix Potter Day, Peru: Independence Day, Singing Telegram Day (1933), World Hepatitis Day, World War I Begins (1914)

29. Lord of the Rings Day, *NASA (1958), *Rain Day

30. Elvis Presley's First Concert (1954), *Emily Brontë (1818), Henry Ford Day, National Chicken and Waffles Day, *Paperback Books (1935), United Nations: International Day of Friendship, United Nations: World Day Against Trafficking in Persons, Vanuatu: Independence Day

31. *US Patent Office Opened (1790)

HOLIDAY MARKETING IDEAS FOR JULY

Photographer: Arianne Leishman

Alopecia Month for Women — This month we recognize the women in our lives who have, for one reason or another, suffered the loss of their luscious mane. Having owned a hair transplant clinic for twenty-three years, I can attest to the total devastation a woman experiences when she loses her hair. Causes of Alopecia are varied, from chemicals and cancer to stress, and yes, even traction Alopecia, for those who braid their hair tightly all too often.

There are a few things you could do to bring awareness to your business through the celebration of this holiday. You might consider a charity drive or volunteering at a hospital or cancer treatment center near you. Alternatively, you could hold a class on how to alleviate stress and the causes of it. Or for young girls, proper haircare techniques, or even a hair and makeup party.

One sure way to get the media's attention is to donate head scarfs, hats, or wigs. Or, if you know a lot of long-locked lasses, you might donate hair. These are just the first things that come to mind when I consider how to focus on this tragic time in a woman's life.

July 1 Postage Stamp Day — Imagine all the fun you will have celebrating this Weird & Wacky holiday. Creating postage stamps to share can be quite inspiring, and creative people will probably savor the chance to showcase their designs. So, have a postage stamp design contest.

Another thing you could do is have a Postage Stamp Sized Swap Party! Very simple things, small, delicate, anything that comes close to the size requirements could be fun to swap or trade. Some of the best parties I have attended had prizes that were pretty weird & wacky.

If you aren't into either of these ideas you can always opt for sending out cards with actual stamps on them to your best customers and clients. Better yet, design your own stamp to make your card even more special.

Jul 3 Caribbean Day — How fun would it be to organize a parade in your city!? This would require a whole new process of speaking with your city manager and proper licensing since it requires traffic rerouting and such, but can be a fun and fabulous way to get your business recognized.

If you aren't up to that big of a task, you can also make it a Caribbean Day dress for the day at your office. Then again, like me, if you are a home based business then you need to consider more interactive on-line activities or card, fliers, or email campaigns.

One fun game you can play at an on-line event might be name that tune type. Another might be a title fill-in-the-blank game. A fill-in-the-blank sample is in the appendix, to make it easy for you. You'll also find a card you can brand and use, as well as a card / envelope size chart if you are up to the task of designing your own.

Jul 7 Bonza Bottler Day — The world over, this Weird & Wacky Holiday has become a favorite! Why? Well, the answer is simply put in one word, "Party." Theme parties are always fun. Look at the month-long holidays and generate your party theme around one of them.

Another sure-to-please way to celebrate is to collect children's gifts in your office or organization to take to children who are in the hospital or have special needs, or everyone can bring canned goods, etc., to distribute to those who are in need.

Best of all, there are no limits. Think up your own party or event theme. After all, that's what this Weird & Wacky Holiday is all about!

Jul 12 Night of Nights — Today, or rather tonight, we commemorate the history of maritime radio and the men and women who, in days gone by, sent and received vital information through the use of this transmitter. It also marks the closing of commercial Morse operations in the USA.

The Maritime Radio Historical Society states, "Once, the maritime mobile bands were populated edge to edge with powerful coast stations operating from virtually every country on every continent. Once, the ships of world trade and the great passenger liners filled the air with their radiograms — and with their calls for help when in danger on the sea. Now those bands are largely silent."

So, think about events that would answer the call for help. The possibilities are endless as throughout the world there are people who are less fortunate than you. Consider a charity drive, or training event. You might even want to have everyone in your office or event wear black to commemorate the death of commercial Morse operations.

Jul 20 Riot Act Day — While you need to take action every day to make your life better, today you are prompted to let anyone who will listen, and some that won't, say what irks you. Tweet about things that bother the heck out of you. Better yet, write a letter to the editor, if the shoe fits.

Share your story, and help other do the same. Every time you speak out for a cause that touches you personally, you take control back from the bully or stupidity of those around you. So, stand up and shout, "I'm mad as hell, and I'm not gonna take it anymore!" Make this the theme of the day, and your post, or event.

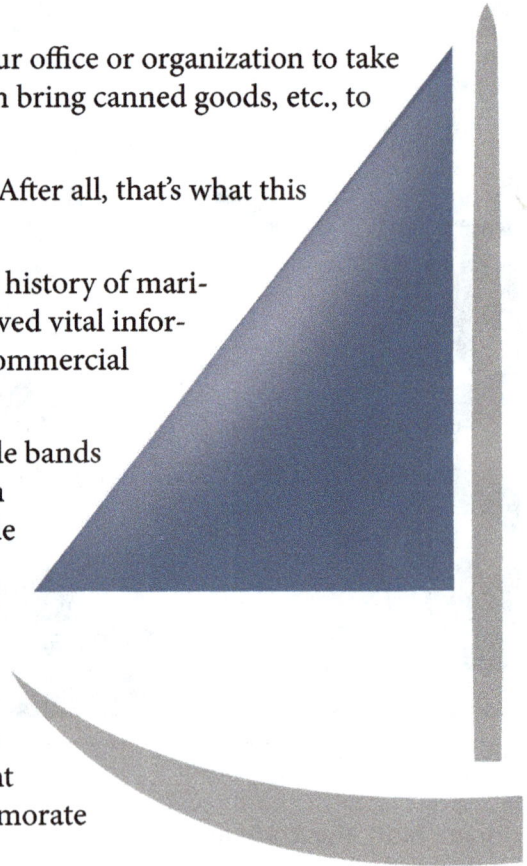

Wear a button on your shoulder with that saying and the blessed day that allows you the freedom to do so. That's the very least you can do. If you can afford to, create buttons to give away or have a 'color your own Riot Act Day button' event. Perhaps you could have a contest to see what others come up with for a button your group can give away or wear on this day. You'll find one I designed for you to make it easy, if you need it, in the appendix.

Jul 29 Rain Day — Rain is one of humanity's life-giving forces. So, let it rain on your parade! Come up with Rain Day quotes to share on social media, or find them on quote sites. If you recall from previous Weird & Wacky Holiday Marketing Guide editions there is a list of quote sites in the appendix to make it easy for you to find appropriate quotes for any occasion. This one is no exception. Some quotes extracted from one of the quote sources can be found there, too.

You could have a poetry contest with the subject of rain or perhaps you could spend the day sharing ideas how your customers or clients can grow personally, or how their businesses can grow. To that end, in the appendix you will find a poster you can use to announce your event. It is clean and simple to allow you to easily remove the text and replace it with your own event information. If you need help with branding it or want something a bit more developed all it takes is a quick email to: support@holidaymarketingguide.com.

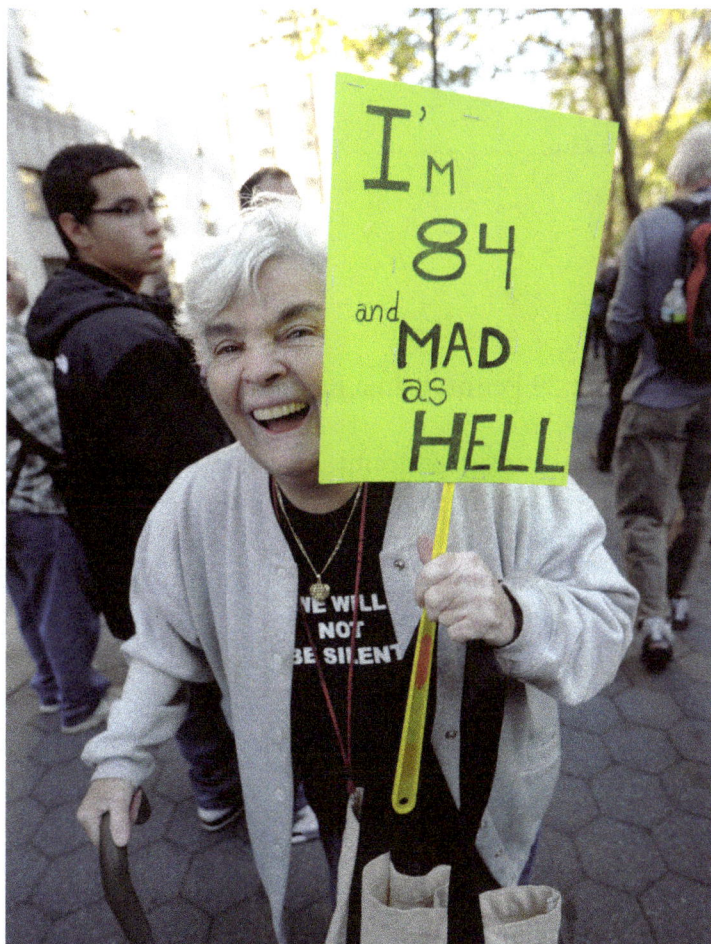

AUGUST

MONTH-LONG HOLIDAYS

Aug 5 – Oct 29 Pennsylvania Renaissance Faire

American Adventures Month, Black Business Month, Boomers Making a Difference Month, Children's Eye Health & Safety Month, Children's Vision & Learning Month, National Immunization Awareness Month, National Spinal Muscular Atrophy Awareness Month, National Traffic Awareness Month, Read-A-Romance Month, Shop On-line for Groceries Month, What Will Be Your Legacy Month

WEEK-LONG HOLIDAYS

Aug 1 – 7 International Clown Week (First full week), National Minority Donor Awareness Week, World Breastfeeding Week

Aug 3 – 13 Wisconsin State Fair

Aug 4 – 13 New Jersey State Fair/Sussex County Farm and Horse Show

Aug 4 – 20 Indiana State Fair

Aug 6 – 12 National Exercise with Your Child Week, National Health Center Week

Aug 7 – 9 Hatfield–McCoy Feud Days

Aug 7 – 11 Exhibitor Appreciation Week, Psychic Week, Weird Contest Week

Aug 7 – 13 Assistance Dog Week, National Bargain Hunting Week

Aug 9 – 13 Perseid Meteor Showers

Aug 10 – 20 Illinois State Fair (tentative), Iowa State Fair, Missouri State Fair

Aug 10 – 13 National Hobo Days

Aug 10 – 19 Skowhegan State Fair

Aug 11 – 19 Elvis Week, West Virginia State Fair

Aug 12 – 17 Mae West Birthday Gala

Aug 15 – 21 National Aviation Week

Aug 17 – 27 Kentucky State Fair (with World's Championship Horse Show), Little League Baseball® World Series

Aug 19 – 25 International Federation of Library Association's Annual Conference

Aug 24 – Sep 4 Alaska State Fair, Hotter 'n Hell Hundred Bike Race, Maryland State Fair, Minnesota State Fair, New York State Fair

Aug 25 – 31 Be Kind to Humankind Week

Aug 25 – Sep 4 Colorado State Fair, Nebraska State Fair, Oregon State Fair

Aug 27 – Sep 4 Burning Man

Aug 31 – Sep 4 South Dakota State Fair

DAILY HOLIDAYS

1. Benin: Independence Day, Colorado Day, Emancipation of 500 Day, *Girlfriend's Day, *Lughnasadh, *Respect for Parents Day, Rounds Resounding Day, *Spiderman Day, Switzerland: Confederation Day, Tisha B'Av or Fast of Ab, United Kingdom: Minden Day, *US Census Day, *US Customs Day, Word Lung Cancer Day, *World Wide Web or Internaut Day (1990)

2. Costa Rica: Feast of Our Lady of Angels, *Declaration of Independence: Official Signing (1776)

3. Columbus Sails for the New World (1492), Niger: Independence Day

4. Braham Pie Day, *Coast Guard Day,* Louis Armstrong Day, Queen Elizabeth, The Queen Mother Birthday, Single Working Woman's Day

5. Croatia: Homeland Thanksgiving Day, Fancy Farm Picnic Day, National Mustard Day

6. American Family Day in Arizona, Bolivia: Independence Day, Death Penalty Day, *Hiroshima Day, Jamaica: Independence Day, *Lucille Ball Day (1911), Sister's Day®

7. Australia: Picnic Day, Colorado Day, Hatfield-McCoy Feud Eruption Day, Jamaica: Independence Day, *Mata Hari Day (1876), National Lighthouse Day, *Particularly Preposterous Packaging Day, *Professional Speakers Day

8. *Bonza Bottler Day™, *Odie Day (1978), *Sneak Some Zucchini Onto Your Neighbor's Porch Night

9. Japan: Moment of Silence (Bombing of Nagasaki), *Moment of Silence Day, Singapore: National Day, South Africa: National Women's Day, *United Nations: International Day of The World's Indigenous People, *Veep Day

10. Candid Camera Day, National S'mores Day, Nestlé Day (1814), *Smithsonian Day

11. *Alex Haley Day (1921), Chadd: Independence Day, Japan: Yama No Hi (Mountain Day), President's Joke Day (1984), Saint Clare of Assisi: Feast Day

12. *Home Sewing Machine Day, *IBM PC Day, Middle Children's Day, National Garage Sale Day, Night of the Murdered Poets,*United Nations: International Youth Day, *Vinyl Record Day

13. *Alfred Hitchcock (1899), *Annie Oakley Day (1860), Berlin Wall Erected (1961), Herbert Hoover Day (Sunday nearest Aug 10th), *International Left Hander's Day

14. Canada: Yukon Discovery Day, *Navajo Nation: Code Talkers Day, *Social Security Day, Victory Day, *V–J Day (1945)

15. *Assumption of the Virgin Mary, *Best Friends Day, *Chauvin Day, Check the Chip Day, India & Korea: Independence Day, *National Relaxation Day, *Panama Canal Day (1914), Transcontinental US Railway Completion (1870), *Woodstock (1969)

16. International Wave at Surveillance Day, *Joe Miller's Joke Day, Klondike Gold Discovery Day, National Roller Coaster Day

17. Balloon Crossing of Atlantic Ocean (1978), *Clinton's "Meaning of 'Is' Is" Day (1998), *Davy Crockett (1786), Gabon & Indonesia: Independence Day, *Mae West (1893)

18. *Bad Poetry Day, *Birth Control Pills Day, *Mail–Order Catalog Day, National Badge Ribbon Day, Serendipity Day

19. Afghanistan: Independence Day, *Black Cow (Root Beer Float) Day, Don Ho Day (1930), International Geocaching Day, International Homeless Animals Day® and Candle-light Vigils, United Nations: World Humanitarian Day

20. Hungary: Saint Stephen's Day, *Plutonium Day

21. *American Bar Association Day, *Poet's Day, Solar Eclipse

22. *Be An Angel Day, *International Yacht Race Day, *Southern Hemisphere Hoodie-Hoo Day, Vietnam Conflict Begins (1945)

23. First Man-Powered Flight (1977), Gene Kelly (1912), *United Nations: Day For The Remembrance of the Slave Trade & Its Abolition, *Valentino Day

24. *Pluto Demoted Day, Ukraine: Independence Day, *Vesuvius Day, William Wilberforce Day

25. Founders Day, International Bat Night, *Kiss–and–Make-Up Day, *National Park Service Day, Uruguay: Independence Day, *Wizard of Oz Day (1939)

26. Baseball Day (First Televised, 1939), *National Dog Day, *Women's Equality Day

27. Moldova: Independence Day, *Mother Teresa Day, *The Duchess Who Wasn't Day

28. China: Double Seven Day, *March on Washington (1963), *Race Your Mouse Around the Icons Day, *Radio Commercials Day

29. *According to Hoyle Day, *More Herbs, Less Salt Day, United Nations: International Day Against Nuclear Tests

30. Huey P Long Day, National Grief Awareness Day, *National Holistic Pet Day, United Nations: International Day of Victims of Enforced Disappearances

31. Kazakhstan: Constitution Day & Independence Day, *Love Litigating Lawyers Day, Malaysia: Freedom Day, Moldova: National Language Day, Trinidad and Tobago: Independence Day

HOLIDAY MARKETING IDEAS FOR AUGUST

Aug 7 – 13 National Bargain Hunting Week — This week is a gift horse dropped in your lap! Your customers and clients are out there looking for sales every day, but even so much more this week. So, don't miss out. Get your business hat on and think of a special you can run that will tease your customers and clients, and everyone else who might be interested, into taking advantage of your offering.

For loyal customers, you could give a taste of something they haven't ordered before that you think, from past purchases, they could very well need or want. Maybe they just didn't know you offered it, or that they needed it. Either way, this has worked for many business owners before you, and there's no reason it can't work for you, too!

When you get a group of business owners together for a big sales bask, you can multiply your reach through each other's customer and client bases. It is truly a win-win-win situation for all involved!

The first web server: this machine was used by Tim Berners-Lee in 1990 to develop and run the first WWW server, multi-media browser and web editor. © CERN, Licence: CC-BY-SA-4.0

Aug 1 World Wide Web Day — Where would we be without the Internet? Do you remember life before computers? Some of you will and some of you won't, but believe me, the world got a whole lot smaller thanks to the Internet being made publicly available for all of us at work and at play.

We use the Web to search for everything, everywhere! No longer do we have to wait for the local store to get a specific item in for us. We just hop on the Internet and push a button and in a matter of days it arrives at our doorstep. And, for those of us in business, we, too, have been able to expand our reach not just nationally, but internationally! Hoorah for the World Wide Web!

The web doesn't just connect machines, it connects people! So, set your sights on an on-line event today to celebrate. Whether that means social media to you, blog tours, webinars, or chatting on Google hangout, be sure to get your fingers poised over the keyboard, turn on your webcam, and use this Weird & Wacky Holiday to your advantage. You will find a card you can use or post on social media, if you like, in the appendix. Happy WWW Day!

Aug 7 Mata Hari Day — Mata Hari, we all have been told, was a double agent for the Germans during WWI. Maybe that's true and maybe not. The Germans may have set her up as retribution for discovering her espionage. Regardless, she came to the same end.

But, at the end of her life, facing the firing squad, she exclaimed, "I have always lived for love and pleasure." And, as the Parisian firing squad readied their weapons to execute their former spy turned accused German double agent, Mata Hari walked directly to her spot and stood face forward. She dismissed her blindfold and looked the gunmen in the eye and blew them a kiss. Now, that to me is a gutsy lady.

Therefore, today we celebrate her life. So, thinking of ways to commemorate her strength of character, your challenge is to help strengthen the lives and businesses of those who look to you for guidance. Sharing the four pillars of a strong character — desire, integrity, confidence, and humility — or participating in seminars, webinars, teleseminars, hangouts, tweets, and posts on social media and blogs are all good ways to accomplish your task.

If you are an author or any writing service or training professional, think about ways to share how to write or publish. Begin with strong character development, move into plot-line, and go from there.

Aug 13 International Left Hander's Day — Today we recognize how inconvenient our right handed world is for left handers. Between 10 and 30% of our population are left handed. These numbers seem trivial until you realize we are talking about a base of over 7 BILLION people!

A fun activity today is to have a Left Hand Zone party. In this area you begin by tying your right hand behind your back and see how you fare. In the appendix, you will find a list of activities you can have your participants perform. Lefthandersday.com provides us with posters to use, which you will find in the appendix. But, they also provide an Infographic titled, "Top Tips for Helping Little Left-Hander's in a Right-Handed World" that I think is worth a look. They recommend you share on your social media. You'll find it here: http://www.lefthandersday.com/teachers/child-info#. WCSUIS0rJR0.

Ruffles
#RoughLife

FINALLY, A CHIP FOR LEFTIES.

For social media enthusiasts, I recommend you tweet with the hashtag they recommend: #lefthandersday. Also, on Pinterest, Facebook, and other image based social media sites you could have a Left Hand Zone photo display.

Aug 18 National Badge Ribbon Day — For the first-time ever, Chase Calendar adds this Weird & Wacky Holiday to their official calendar. So, in honor of Nick Topitzes, Founder of pc/nametag®'s achievement, we, too, have chosen to recognize this holiday for your use in promoting your business, or just for having some fun.

Nick states, "A bit of levity can raise smiles at a meeting — and also raise some money for an organization. As our stack-a-ribbon® award fun titles have done. Stock up on a variety of our badge ribbons with witty sayings (like 'Bored Member,' 'Got Reviews?' and 'Insignificant Other') and offer them for sale at your registration table. It's a great way to raise funds and give attendees a conversation starter. At just a buck or two, the ribbons can bring in hundreds of dollars. As another fun title says, 'Cool!'"

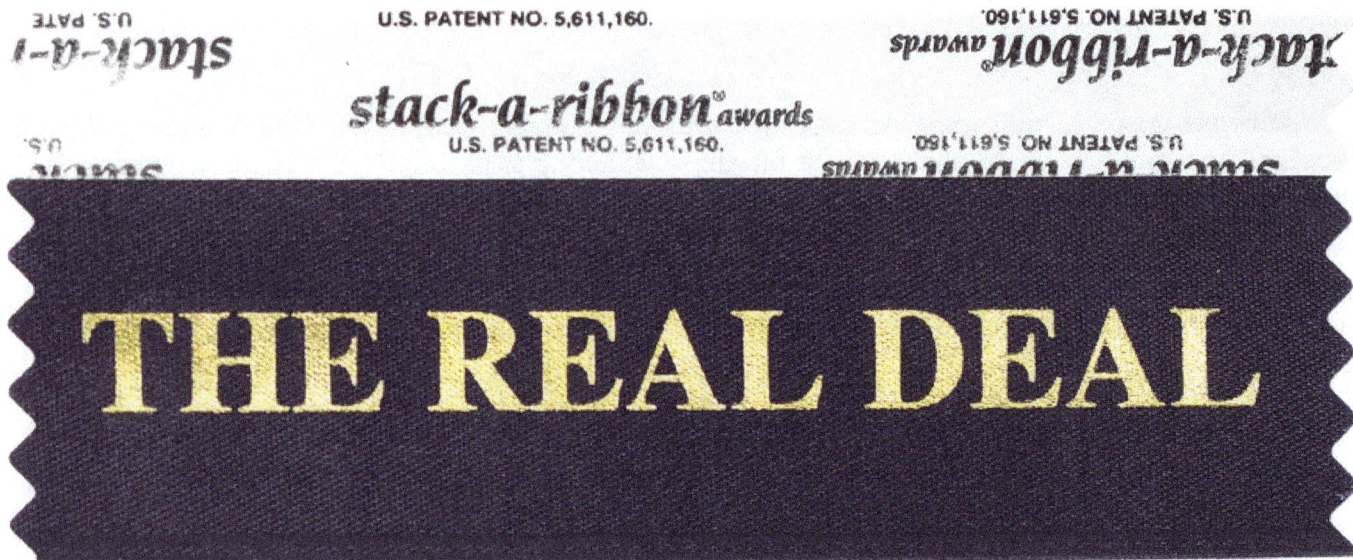

stack-a-r

stack-a-ribbon® awards

U.S. PATENT NO. 5,611,160.

U.S. PATENT NO. 5,611,160.

tack-a-ribbon® awards

U.S. PATENT NO. 5,611,160.

THE REAL DEAL

Share your ideas for badge ribbon sayings. Contact Nick and hold a contest. Winner gets their badge ribbon added to their catalog! Be sure to share the link to their catalog to ensure your saying isn't already being used. There are a lot of Weird & Wacky badges to choose from already, so I have listed the link to their catalog in the appendix.

Aug 28 Race Your Mouse Around the Icons Day — I know you've never done this, but I certainly have. When your computer is slow to load, or when you're waiting for something to happen, you jiggle, move, wiggle your mouse around, like it is gonna make any difference at all! Ha, I thought so. Guilty as charged.

Cleaning your mouse, and even your mouse pad, before you get started is advised. You want to make sure it moves smoothly, right? You could also share tips on how to clean them or even have folks post photos of their mouse's backside grime. I know, eww, but it could make them aware and they'll be glad they did once the cleaning is complete.

Sending out special eCards wishing your customers and clients a Happy Race Your Mouse Around the Icons Day to let them know you are thinking about them. Remember, when you touch your customers and clients in fun and frivolous ways, they will think fondly of you and may even remember you when they need your products or services.

Feel free to use this graphic I created for your use. And, be sure to brand it to your needs. You'll find a larger version in the appendix.

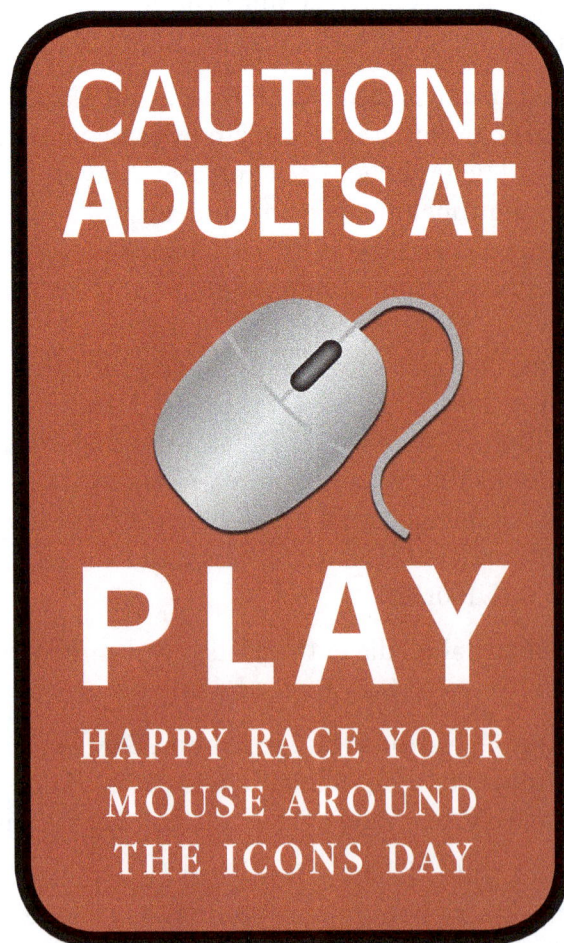

CAUTION! ADULTS AT PLAY

HAPPY RACE YOUR MOUSE AROUND THE ICONS DAY

SEPTEMBER

MONTH-LONG HOLIDAYS

Sep 8 – 10 Oktoberfest (Covington, KY)
Sep 7 – 18 Paralympic Games
Sep 15 – Oct 15 National Hispanic Heritage Month
Sep 16 – Oct 1 Oktoberfest
Sep 15 – Oct 1 The Big E
Sep 15 – Oct 15 National Hispanic Heritage Month
Sep 26 – Oct 1 Banned Books Week — Celebrating the Freedom to Read

Atrial Fibrillation Month, Attention Deficit Disorder Month, Be Kind To Editors & Writers Month, Childhood Cancer Awareness Month, Chili: National Month, Fall Hat Month, Great American Low–Cholesterol, Low–fat Pizza Bake Month, Gynecology Cancer Awareness Month, Happy Cat Month, Hunger Action Month, Intergeneration Month, International Women's Friendship Month, Library Card Sign–up Month, National Bake and Decorate Month, National Childhood Obesity Awareness Month, National DNA, Genomics & Stem Cell Education Month, National Head Lice Prevention Month, National Honey Month, National Mushroom Month, National Ovarian Cancer Awareness Month, National Preparedness Month, National Prostate Cancer Awareness Month, National Recovery Month, National Rice Month, National Service Dog Month, National Skin Care Awareness Month, National Wilderness Month, One-on–One Month, Ovarian Cancer Awareness Month, September is Healthy Aging® Month, Shameless Promotion Month, Sports Eye Health & Safety Month, Subliminal Communications Month, Update Your Resume Month, Worldwide Speak Out Month

WEEK-LONG HOLIDAYS

Sep 1 – 4 Woodstock

Sep 1 – 7 Brazil: Independence Week, Self-University Week

Sep 1 – 24 Washington State Fair

Sep 2 – 5 Great Fire of London (1666)

Sep 2 – 9 Eastern Idaho State Fair

Sep 3 – 9 National Waffle Week, Substitute Teacher Appreciation Week

Sep 4 – 8 National Payroll Week

Sep 4 – 10 National Suicide Prevention Week

Sep 4 – 11 National Stearman Fly-In

Sep 7 – 17 New Mexico State Fair, Utah State Fair

Sep 8 – 17 Kansas State Fair, Tennessee State Fair

Sep 9 – 10 Sodbuster Days

Sep 10 – 16 National Assisted Living Week

Sep 11 – 17 America's Largest RV Show (Hershey, PA)

Sep 11 – 16 National Line Dance Week

Sep 13 – 16 American Massage Therapy Association® National Convention (Pasadena. CA)

Sep 14 – 24 Oklahoma State Fair

Sep 11 – 23 Build a Better Image Week

Sep 17 – 23 Constitution Week, International Clean Hands Week, National Farm Safety and Health Week, National Historically Black Colleges and Universities Week (tentative), National Rehabilitation Awareness Celebration Week, National Security Officer Appreciation Week, National Singles Week, Prostate Cancer Awareness Week, Tolkien Week

Sep 18 – 24 Balance Awareness Week, International Women's eCommerce Days

Sep 24 – 30 Banned Books Week — Celebrating the Freedom to Read, International Week of the Deaf, World Reflexology Week

Sep 29 – Oct 8 Virginia State Fair

Sep 29 – Oct 22 Texas State Fair

DAILY HOLIDAYS

1. Bring Your Manners to Work Day, *Chicken Boy's Birthday, *Edgar Rice Burroughs (1875) *Emma M. Nutt Day, International Toy Tips Executive Toy Test Day, Orthodox Ecclesiastical New Year, Slovakia: Constitution Day, Titanic Discovery Day, Uzbekistan: Independence Day, WWII Begins (1939)

2. *Bison–Ten Yell Day, Calendar Adjustment Day, US Treasury Department Founded Day, Vietnam: Independence Day, *V–J Day

3. Penny Press Day (1833), Qatar: Independence Day

4. Canada & US: Labor Day (first Monday in September), Curaçao: Animal's Day, Electric Lights Day, Great Bathtub Race Day, Mackinac Bridge Walk, *Newspaper Carrier Day, *Paul Harvey Day

5. Be Late for Something Day, United Nations: International Day of Charity

6. Baltic States: Independence Day, Jane Addams Day, Swaziland: Independence Day, United Nations: Millennium Summit (1955)

7. Brazil: Independence Day, England: Queen Elizabeth I Birthday (1533), *Google Commemoration Day (1998), *Grandma Moses Day, *Neither Snow nor Rain Day–Day

8. Huey P. Long Shot Day, Macedonia: Independence Day, National Day of Prayer and Remembrance, National Dog Walker Appreciation Day, Pediatric Hematology/Oncology Nurses Day, Tarzan Day, *United Nations: International Literacy Day

9. *Bonza Bottler Day™, Japan: Chrysanthemum Day, Prairie Day, Richmond's Outlaw Days, Tajikistan: Independence Day, *Wonderful Weirdos Day

10. National Grandparents' Day, National Hug Your Hound Day, Swap Ideas Day, World Suicide Prevention Day

11. *Attack on America Day, Ethiopia: New Year's Day, *Food Stamps Day, National Boss/Employee Exchange Day, *Patriot Day and National Day of Service and Remembrance

12. Defenders Day, United Nations: Opening Day of General Assembly, United Nations: Day for South-South Cooperation

13. Kids Take Over the Kitchen Day, *National Celiac Awareness Day, Roald Dahl Day, Scooby Doo Day

14. *Solo Transatlantic Balloon Crossing (1984)

15. *Agatha Christie Day, *Constitution/Pledge Across America Day, Costa Rica: Independence Day, El Salvador: Independence Day, *First National Convention for Blacks (1830), *Greenpeace Day (1971), Guatemala & Honduras: Independence Day, National POW/MIA Recognition (the third Friday in September), National Tradesmen Day, Nicaragua: Independence Day, Quarterly Estimated Federal Income Tax Payers' Due Date (also Jan 17, Apr 17, June 15, and Sep 15, 2015), United Kingdom: Battle of Britain Day, *United Nations: International Day of Democracy

16. *Anne Bradstreet Day, Big Whopper Liar's Contests Day, Cherokee Strip Day, General Motors Day, *Great Seal of the US (1782), International Coastal Cleanup Day, Locate an Old Friend Day, Mayflower Day, Mexico: Independence Day, Papua New Guinea: Independence Day, *United Nations: International Day for the Preservation of the Ozone Layer, World Play-Doh Day

17. *Citizenship Day, *Constitution Day (1787), National Constitution Center Constitution Day, National Football League Formed Day (1920), VFW Ladies Auxiliary Day

18. Chili: Independence Day, Japan: Respect for the Aged Day, National HIV/AIDS and Aging Awareness Day, *US Air Force Birthday, *US Capitol Cornerstone Laid, White Woman Made American Indian Chief Day

19. *"Iceman" Mummy Discovered (1991), *International Talk Like A Pirate Day, IT Professionals Day, Saint Christopher (Saint Kitts) and Nevis: Independence Day

20. *Billie Jean King Wins Battle of the Sexes, (1973), *National Equal Rights Founded (1884), National School Backpack Awareness Day, Rosh Hashanah Begins at Sundown

21. Armenia, Belize & Malta: Independence Day, Islamic New Year, Little Brown Jug Day, National Surgical Technologists Day, Rosh Hashanah or Jewish New Year, *United Nations: International Day of Peace

22. America Business Women's Day, Dear Diary Day, *Emancipation Proclamation (1862), Hobbit Day, Ice Cream Cone Day, International Day of Radiant Peace, Long Count Day (1927), Mabon (Alban Elfed), Mali: Independence Day, National Centarian's Day, National Walk 'n' Roll Dog Day, US Postmaster General's Day (1789)

23. Baseball's Greatest Dispute Day, *Celebrate Bisexuality Day, Checkers Day, Fish Amnesty Day, Innergize Day, *Lewis & Clark Expedition Returns (1806), National Hunting and Fishing Day, National Public Lands Day, Planet Neptune Discovery (1846), R.E.A.D. in America Day

24. Gold Star Mother's and Family Day, Guinea-Bissau: Independence Day, International Day of the Deaf, *National Punctuation Day

25. Family Day—Be Involved, Stay Involved™ Day, *First American Newspaper Published (1690), *Greenwich Mean Time Begins (1676), *National One-Hit Wonder Day, Pacific Ocean Discovered (1513)

26. *Johnny Appleseed Day

27. *Ancestor Appreciation Day, National Women's Health & Fitness Day, *Samuel Adams (1722), Saint Vincent DePaul Feast Day, *World Tourism Day

28. *Cabrillo Day, Taiwan: Confucius and Teachers' Day, UK: National Poetry Day, United Nations: World Maritime Day, United Nations: World Rabies Day

29. Buffalo Roundup Day, Dow Jones Biggest Drop Day, Hug A Vegan Day, *Michelangelo Antonio (1912), Michaelmas, *National Attend Your Grandchild's Birth Day, National Biscotti Day, National Coffee Day, Scotland Yard Day (1829), Veterans of Foreign Wars Day, Yom Kippur Begins at Sundown

30. Botswana: Independence Day, Fall Astronomy Day, Family Health and Fitness Day–USA®, Gutenberg Bible Published (1452), International Translation Day, Yom Kippur or Day of Atonement

HOLIDAY MARKETING IDEAS FOR SEPTEMBER

Worldwide Speak Out Month—Do you shy away from speaking in public? Perhaps you are a speaker or communications trainer. There's no better time than the month of September to get or give help in this area. Whether you choose a large group forum or you prefer the small group setting, these events can be held live or virtually, and will benefit all in attendance. Building self-esteem and improving speaking skills are two topics you could address at your event. You might also consider any topic that empowers your customers and clients in areas where they need direction.

You could extend the training for the whole month, by offering one session per week, or you could participate in a huge one-time event.

Even products that enable your customers to free up time or make their life or job easier can be reasons to promote this month-long holiday. What about teaching young women proper dress or make-up techniques? For the guys, you could teach them proper dating etiquette. Well, you get the idea. Keep your thinking cap on and I'm sure you'll come up with a way to promote your products or services this month.

Sep 17–23 International Clean Hands Week—"Clean hands prevent illness and save lives!" This week highlights the various activities people and communities can participate in to improve hygiene. Start out with the obvious; healthcare professionals, school nurses, and health and fitness coaches who would speak on this subject. Then there are always fliers, tweets, and posts that are accomplished with ease.

Trial size bottles of hand sanitizer with your business card attached might be the perfect solution to show your business support for this effort. If you aren't into giving them out in line in the grocery store, then perhaps you can find a restaurant to partner with to help sponsor and distribute the bottles. I believe you can also get the sanitizer bottles themselves branded through specialty gift stores.

In the appendix I place "The Four Principals Of Hand Awareness" and a cute mascot for HenrytheHand.com. Also, in the resources section of the appendix you will find a link to some superb graphics you can use for free, through Cleaning institute. I highly recommend taking the time to review all the tools they have to help you in your quest for cleanliness training.

Sep 2 Bison–Ten Yell Day— Today's Weird & Wacky Holiday is supposed to be the bicentennial birthday of a fictitious person. In reality it's all one giant (and bad) pun, get it? Bison-Ten-Yell, said just right, sounds a lot like "bicentennial."

Anyway, since the 200-year old birthday boy or girl is fictitious, he or she never really existed—she or he was never actually born—I guess that makes it okay for him or her to have a different birth date every year!

So, why on earth do we celebrate the bicentennial birthday of a person who never existed? Today is supposed to honor the person who invented ten verbal signals that could be yelled during a war to alert one's soldiers to the battle plan. Ten signals, yelled signals—these are the reasons given for the "Ten-Yell" part of the name. The

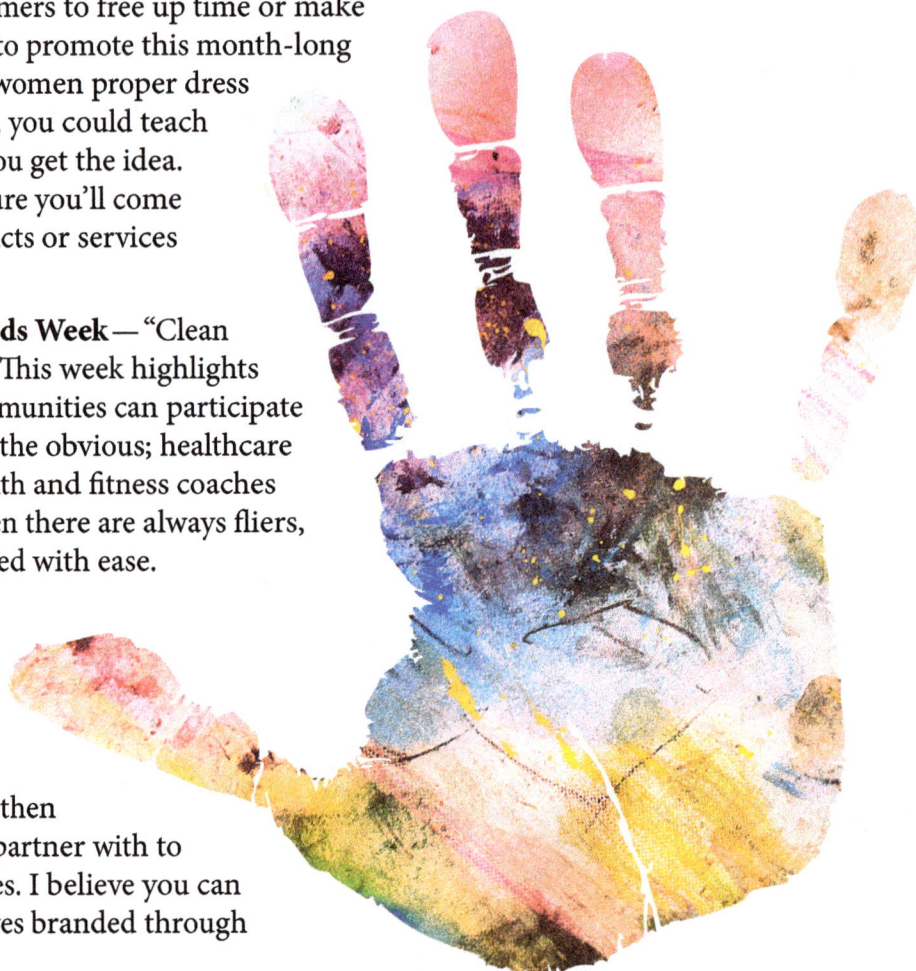

soldiers had to memorize the meaning of each signal. Obviously, a commander yelling something that everyone could understand wouldn't be very effective — because then the enemy would know the plan, too! So the soldiers on one side would be taught their signals, and the soldiers on the other side would be taught their completely different signals. And everyone hoped that the enemy didn't figure out their code.

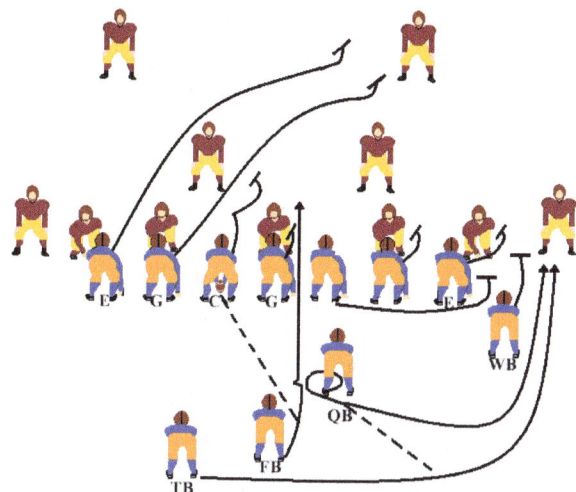

Today, to celebrate, create your own code. Share it with your friends and 'code talk' to each other throughout the day. Sounds like a fun party to me. Heck, all work and no play makes for one very dull life! So, go have some fun and pass the word around. You never know if your team's secret code will be the one that becomes the next hot fad. After all, it is a birthday party we're celebrating. Isn't it? Look for a card you can use to share in the appendix. Make it into a greeting card or postcard and send it snail mail to your best customers and clients with a personalized note from you.

Sep 4 Electric Lights Day — Today in 1882 New York City became electrified for the first time. And, one of the first buildings to be lit up was the NY Times Building. It is the day that is considered the beginning of the electrical age. And, for me and you that is quite significant when you think about how we suffer when we lose electricity for even a brief moment.

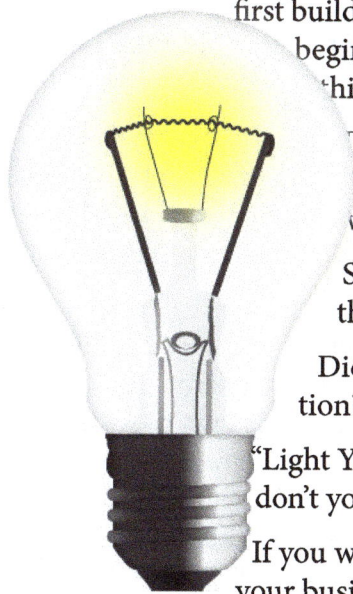

Think about the last time you were sitting at your computer and there was a power surge. Here in Florida it happens all too often! If you haven't recently saved your work, well, that's just too bad.

So, because of the importance of electricity in our lives I think you would agree that this Weird & Wacky Holiday deserves to lighten our path today.

Did I just say something that made your eyes light up? Or spark a thought or imagination? I hope so.

"Light Your Path to Success" would be a superb theme for you Electric Lights Day Event, don't you agree?

If you want something easy to do, simply use social media or eCards to shine a light on your business.

Sep 9 Wonderful Weirdos Day — Get out and celebrate being different, strange, and AWESOME! Today is the day to celebrate personality quirks and your independent spirit.

HowStuffWorks offers a few ways to highlight your inner quirks:

- Become a member of the Ministry of Silly Walks for the day. With each step, swing your legs forward as high as possible. Improvise with random jigs and stutters.

- Create a fake language between friends, something like Pig Latin or Klingon. Ride around public transportation and speak your new language audibly.

- Wearing a silly costume is a reliable way to celebrate weirdness. Go all out with your favorite pirate or superhero costume. If you prefer weirdo minimalism, wearing slinky eyeball spectacles or beagle puss eyeglasses are great ways to highlight any subtle eccentricities. Knee socks of alternate colors and loud, obnoxious patterns are also a plus.

These are merely suggestions. The best way to celebrate Wonderful Weirdos Day is to be your typically weird self, muttering on elevators and dancing through crosswalks.

What I suggest for your celebration is be sure to take lots of photos and share them on social media. Set up a page dedicated to this day and invite your friends, family, customers, and clients to participate. You might even give a prize for the best in a couple different categories and one grand prize for the overall winner. You'll find a poster you can use to announce your fun event in the appendix. No matter how you decide to promote your business with this fun day, I wish you a Weird & Wacky Holiday!

Sep 15 Greenpeace Day — Founded in 1971 by 17 activists protesting nuclear testing off the shores of Alaska, Greenpeace now boasts a worldwide membership. Taking on environmental issues and raising awareness, their campaigns continually strive to support and preserve the Earth. This is a subject we all should embrace!

So, show your concern for the environment by getting out there and doing something with a group of other local concerned citizens. In Florida, where I live, that means beach clean-up. However, in your community it may just be your neighborhood or adopted street in your city. While you are at it, be sure to put up posters to let others know to join you. Radio interviews beforehand as well as local TV and newspapers will come on board, if you let them know. Use your press release to announce it to them and call your radio talk shows.

Podcasts, email campaigns, and cards are the simple way share if you don't have the wherewithal to be able to participate or sponsor a local event.

Sep 21 Little Brown Jug Day — The founders of The Jug, Hank Thomson & Joe Neville, had an idea and went for it and now it has grown to become the most prestigious three-year-old, harnessed, pacing horse race in North America.

So, as we look to how to interpret a dream become reality for Thomson & Neville, you could focus activities and events to share and exchange ideas, demonstrate skills, exhibit products, and break barriers. All of these, or just even one, could be accomplished both on-line and off-line.

For your event to become a one-time event is just fine. But, like Hank Thomson & Joe Neville, why not make it an annual event? Who knows how big it will become? It may not reach the level of prestige that Little Brown Jug has, however, you are sure to garner attention of customers, clients, and friends, and maybe even the media, if you just stay focused on the pursuit of success training and giving of your time and talents for other's benefit.

OCTOBER

MONTH-LONG HOLIDAYS

Oct 15 – Nov 30 Wishbone for Pets Days
Oct 24 – Nov 11 World Origami Days

Adopt A Shelter Dog Month, American Cheese Month, Antidepressant Death Awareness Month, Breast Cancer Awareness Month, Caffeine Addiction Recovery Month, Celebrating The Bilingual Child Month, Celiac Disease Awareness Month, Church Library Month, Co-op Awareness Month, Domestic Violence Awareness Month, Dyslexia Awareness Month, Emotional Intelligence Month, Gay & Lesbian History Month, German–American Heritage Month, Global Diversity Awareness Month, Go Hog Wild — Eat Country Ham Month, Health Literacy Month, Home Eye Safety Month, National Arts and Humanities Month, National Audiology Awareness Month, National Breast Cancer Awareness Month, National Bullying Prevention Awareness Month, National Chiropractic Month, National Crime Prevention Month, National Cyber Security Awareness Month, National Dental Hygiene Month, National Depression Education & Awareness Month, National Disability Employment Awareness Month, National Domestic Violence Awareness Month, National Down Syndrome Awareness Month, National "Gain The Inside Advantage" Month, National Kitchen and Bath Month, National Liver Awareness Month, National Medical Librarian Month, National Orthodontic Health Month, National Physical Therapy Month, National Popcorn Poppin' Month, National Reading Group Month, National Roller Skating Month, National Spina Bifida Awareness Month, National Stamp Collecting Month, National Stop Bullying Month, National Work and Family Month, Organize Your Medical Information Month, Photographer Appreciation Month, Polish American Heritage Month, Positive Attitude Month, Rett Syndrome Awareness Month, Spinach Lovers Month, Squirrel Awareness & Appreciation Month, Talk About Prescriptions Month, Vegetarian Month, Workplace Politics Awareness Month, World Menopause Month

WEEK-LONG HOLIDAYS

Oct 1 – 7 Mental Illness Awareness Week, Mystery Series Week, National Carry a Tune Week, National Work from Home Week

Oct 2 – 6 Kids' Goal Setting Week, National Heimlich Heroes Week

Oct 4 – 15 Mississippi State Fair

Oct 4 – 10 United Nations: World Space Week

Oct 5 – 15 Georgia National Fair

Oct 5 – 11 Sukkot, Succoth or Feast of Tabernacles

Oct 6 – 8 Coin, Jewelry, & Stamp Expo (Anaheim, CA)

Oct 6 – 14 Canada: Kitchener-Waterloo Oktoberfest

Oct 7 – 9 Chowder Days

Oct 8 – 14 Earth Science Week, Emergency Nurses Week, Fire Prevention Week, Getting the World to Beat a Path to Your Door Week, National Metric Week, Teen Read Week

Oct 8 – 21 Brazil: Cirio de Nazare

Oct 9 – 13 National School Lunch Week

Oct 10 – 17 Take Your Medicine Americans Week

Oct 11 – 15 Germany: Frankfurt Book Fair

Oct 11 – 22 South Carolina State Fair

Oct 12 – 22 North Carolina State Fair

Oct 12-26 Chicago International Film Festival

Oct 13 – 15 Apple Butter Makin' Days, Southern Festival of Books: A Celebration of the Written Word

Oct 13 – Nov 5 Arizona State Fair (tentative)

Oct 13 – 22 Arkansas State Fair and Livestock Show (tentative)

Oct 15 – 21 Bullying Bystanders Unite Week

Oct 15 – 20 Japan: Newspaper Week

Oct 15 – 21 National Character Counts Week, National Food Bank Week, National Forest Products Week

Oct 17 – 24 Food and Drug Interaction Education and Awareness Week

Oct 21 – 23 India: Diwali (Deepavali)

Oct 22 – 28 National Chemistry Week, National Massage Therapy Awareness Week®, Pastoral Care Week, Rodent Awareness Week

Oct 23 – 27 Nuclear Science Week

Oct 24 – 30 United Nations: Disarmament Week

Oct 24 – 31 Prescription Errors Education & Awareness Week

Oct 25 – 31 International Magic Week

Oct 26 – Nov 12 Louisiana State Fair

Oct 28 – 29 Alabama Renaissance Faire

DAILY HOLIDAYS

1. Blessing of the Fishing Fleet, Country Inn/Bed–and–Breakfast Day, Cyberspace Day, Cyprus: Independence Day, *Fire Pup Day, Model-T Day, Nigeria: Independence Day, *United Nations: International Day of Older Persons, World Communion Sunday, World Vegetarian Day

2. Blue Shirt Day™, Child Health Day (always issued for the first Monday in October), *Guardian Angels Day, *Groucho Marx (1890), Guinea: Independence Day, *National Custodial Workers Day, *"Peanuts" Debut Day (1950), *Phileas Fogg's Wager Day, United Nations: International Day of Nonviolence, United Nations: World Habitat Day

3. Captain Kangaroo Day, Germany: Day of German Unity, Korea: Tangun Day (National Foundation Day), *Mickey Mouse Club Day (1955)

4. *Dick Tracy Day (1931), *Georgian Calendar Adjustment Day, Lesotho: Independence Day, National Ships-In-Bottles Day, Saint Francis of Assisi: Feast Day, *Ten-Four Day

5. National Depression Screening Day, *United Nations: World Teachers Day

6. *American Library Association Founding Day (1876), Egypt: Armed Forces Day, Ireland: Ivy Day, *Jackie Mayer Rehab Day, National Diversity Day, *National German-American Day, World Smile Day, Yom Kippur War

7. National Forgiveness Day, Woofstock

8. *Alvin C. York Day, Grandmother's Day in Florida, *Great Chicago Fire (1871), National Pierogy Day, National Salmon Day, Samoa and American Samoa: White Sunday

9. American Indian Heritage Day, Canada: Thanksgiving Day, Columbus Day (Observed & Traditional), Discovery Day in Hawaii, Fiji: Independence Day, *Leif Erickson Day, Japan: Health–Sports Day, Korea: Hangul (Alphabet Day), National Kick Butt Day, Native Americans' Day, Uganda: Independence Day, *United Nations: World Post Day, Virgin Islands-Puerto Rico Friendship Day, Yorktown Victory Day

10. ADA Lovelace Day, *Bonza Bottler Day™, *Double 10 Day, International Face Your Fears Day, National Handbag Day, *Tuxedo Day, *US Naval Academy Day, World Child Development Day, World Day Against the Death Penalty, *World Mental Health Day

11. *Adding Machine Day, Emergency Nurses Day, *General Pulaski Memorial Day, International Top Spinning Day, National Bring Your Teddy Bear To Work Day, *National Coming Out Day, National Fossil Day, National Stop Bullying Day, National Take Your Parents to Lunch Day, Southern Food Heritage Day, United Nations: International Day of the Girl Child

12. Bahamas Discovery Day, Belize: Columbus Day, Columbus Day (Traditional), *Day of the Six–Billion, Equatorial Guinea: Independence Day, *International Moment of Frustration Scream Day, Mexico: Dia de la Raza, Shemini Atzeret

13. *Leroy Brown Day, *Navy Birthday, Silly Sayings Day, Simchat Torah, United Nations: International Day for Natural Disaster Reduction, US Navy Day

14. *Be Bald and Be Free Day, Monster Myths by Moonlight, Sound Barrier Broken (1947), Supersonic Skydive Day, (2012), Universal Music Day

15. AIDS Walk Atlanta & 5-K Run, *Blind Americans Equality Day (formerly White Cane Safety Day), First Manned Flight (1783), National Cake Decorating Day, National Grouch Day, National Latino AIDS Awareness Day, United Nations: International Day of Rural Women

16. American Department Store Day, Dictionary Day, Birth Control Day (1916), Million Man March (1995), *National Boss' Day, United Nations: World Food Day

17. Black Poetry Day, Evel Knievel Day, *Mulligan Day, San Francisco 1989 Earthquake (1989), *United Nations: International Day for the Eradication of Poverty, 300 Millionth American Born (2006)

18. Alaska Day, Azerbaijan: Independence Day, Canada: Persons Day, Comic Strip Day, Hagfish Day, Missouri Day, Saint Luke Feast Day, Water Pollution Control Day, *World Menopause Day

19. Evaluate Your Life Day, Get to Know Your Customers Day (third Thursday of each quarter is set aside to get to know your customers even better), Get Smart About Credit Day, LGBT Center Awareness Day, National Mammography Day, Yorktown Day

20. Bela Lugosi or Dracula Day, Miss America Rose Day

21. Birth of the Bab, *Incandescent Lamp Day, Sweetest Day

22. Birth of Baha'u'llah, *International Stuttering Awareness Day, Mother-in-Law Day, Smart is Cool Day, World's End Day

23. Hungary: Republic Day (Declares Independence), *IPod Day, National Mole Day, New Zealand: Labor Day, Swallows Depart from San Juan Capistrano, Zambia: Independence Day

24. First Barrel Jump over Niagara Falls (1901), United Nations Day, *United Nations: World Development Information Day

25. Picasso Day, Saint Crispin's Day

26. Austria: National Day, Erie Canal Day, Gunfight at the O.K. Corral (1881), Mule Day

27. *Cranky Coworkers Day, Frankenstein Friday, *Navy Day, Saint Vincent and the Grenadines: Independence Day, United Nations: World Day for Audiovisual Heritage, *Walt Disney Day

28. China: Chung Yeung (Double Nine), Czech Republic: Independence Day, Greece: Ochi Day, Make a Difference Day, *Saint Jude's Day, Statue of Liberty Dedication (1886)

29. European Union: Daylight Savings Time Ends, *Internet Created (1969), National Cat Day, Reformation Sunday

30. Checklists Day, *Create A Great Funeral Day, Devil's Night, *Emily Post Day, *Haunted Refrigerator Night, National Candy Corn Day, "War of the Worlds" (1938) World Audio Drama Day

31. *Books For Treats Day, *Halloween, *Magic Day, Mount Rushmore Day, *National Knock–Knock Day, *Reformation Day, Samhain, Trick or Treat or Beggar's Night, United Nations: World Cities Day

HOLIDAY MARKETING IDEAS FOR OCTOBER

National Work and Family Month — How is the work-life effectiveness of you, your customers, and your clients? This October is the perfect time to fine tune your plan. Devote the month to assisting others finding the perfect work/life balance. This may help you succeed and stay stress-free. By not focusing too long and hard on one or the other, you have a better chance to keep moving in a positive direction.

Organizers, diet & health professionals, lifestyle & business coaches, physical trainers & therapists of all types are the first people you could partner with to share with your customers and clients. Then, we have a whole other group that could be good candidates for your event. Think stress related or health and beauty professionals, even color consultants, guidance counselors, recruiters, relationship counselors, candle and scent reps, meal planners, and the list goes on. Now you can clearly see you could easily fill the month with activities to showcase your business for National Work and Family Month.

Popular weekly themes could include financial education, volunteerism, dependent care, elder care, wellness, stress reduction, and workplace flexibility.

There are cards and emails, podcasts, interviews, live and on-line events, tweets, Facebook posts, Pinterest photos, Google hangouts, and many other ways to keep your business in the eye of your adoring public.

Oct 2 Phileas Fogg's Wager Day — Today launches the famous, albeit fictional, bet that Jules Verne wrote about in his novel, *Around the World in 80 Days*. Circling the globe was an impossible feat, a long time ago. But, today our words and businesses circle the globe and come back again to us in record time. We even can visit with each other no matter where we are located in the world via live time computer chat.

So, to celebrate this holiday, invite one and all to get an on-line connection and share your thoughts and ideas for the benefit of those who attend your event. Perhaps you have been inspired by the book to virtually circle the globe in 80 days. Just plot a course and timeline, and enjoy the "trip" with books, videos, games, recipes, and maybe even costumes representing each culture you visit!

Remember, there are always cards, emails, and social media postings that are available as promotional tools for the faint of heart who aren't ready to step out of their comfort zones and soar to new heights.

Oct 8 National Salmon Day — Today we celebrate one of my all-time favorite fish, the salmon. This fish gives its life for its offspring. And, it swims against the current to do so. So, there's no better day to celebrate your

upstream battle in business. It's never easy to be a committed, small business owner. So, today honor those who not are doing just that, but those who successfully manage to make it up stream and dedicate their time and knowledge to giving back from their storehouses of information and knowledge.

If you have a mentor who has helped you in the past, or even is currently helping, send them a note to wish them a Happy National Salmon Day! And, if you are a mentor, spend the day sharing in an event that will touch the lives of others who are seeking ways to stay the course.

It's not always an easy stream to swim in, sharks are lurking and the water is not always clear. But, with guts, determination, and a little bit of help up the salmon ladder, you, too, can reach your goals.

Oct 11 National Fossil Day — What is a fossil? It is a permanent impression of plants or animals preserved in stone or other material. This suggests finding ways to make your own impression on the world around you. Some ways you can do this are by sharing a smile or a kind word with those whose lives you touch today.

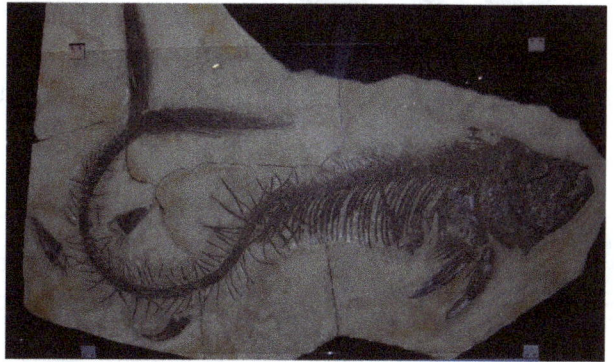

Fossil_Xiphactinus_audax By Totodu74 [Public domain], via Wikimedia Commons

It is also about discovery, and carefully examining the world around you to discover hidden treasures, and then studying them even more carefully to see the tiniest of details. This then suggests perhaps reviewing your business' mission statement or any part of your business that needs attention. If it needs a bit of brushing off or restoration, now is the time to bring it to light and carve a new, clearer image of your business' future.

Whether you chose to do this on your own or in a group setting with the help of others, the choice is yours. But, if you do decide to host a National Fossil Day event, be sure to include at least one fun activity for your attendees. Be sure to check out the resources section of the appendix for the link to the National Park Services National Fossil Day offerings and event listings.

Additionally, I have designed a National Fossil Day poster to make it easy for you to announce your event, obtain sponsors, and brand to your own business needs. You will find a copy in the appendix.

Oct 18 Comic Strip Day — Just for the fun of it, we celebrate Comic Strip Day. There were cartoons before but never an official comic strip until this date in 1896 called "The Yellow Kid Takes a Hand at Golf". So, to celebrate this Weird & Wacky Holiday, take a hand at creating your own comic strip and posting your efforts on-line. Have a Comic Strip Day contest and share the frivolity. Sometimes you just have to play to regenerate or take the time to connect with your audience.

Oct 21 Sweetest Day — Today is a day to share romantic deeds or expressions such as giving presents or greeting cards and candy to loved ones. Similar to Valentine's Day to me, you will find ways to show you care to your best and most loyal customers and clients a sure-fire, fabulous way to ingratiate yourself and your business to them.

Whether you chose to send a card or present them with a sweet treat, it will be gladly accepted and you know that will endear them to you even more than before. Heck, why not take this chance to send a little something to your clients who are on the fence or who you haven't heard from in a while? Keeping your name in front of them is what you need to do, so they will remember you and your great customer service when they need your help.

Another idea is to take after the founders of Sweetest Day and distribute candy to orphanages and low-income homes in your area. The efforts of the founders saw the candy was distributed among 26 local charities. Two-hundred twenty-five children were given candy in the chapel at the Society for Prevention of Cruelty to Children, and Big Sisters of America Group.

If you opt for this way to celebrate, absolutely let the media know and you and your fellow donors and sponsors will become overnight media darlings, perhaps even nationally!

I'M PURRRFECT FOR YOU!

Oct 29 National Cat Day — Celebrated annually, National Cat Day is the most popular holiday for cats and cat lovers. It encourages adoption and floods the Internet with cuteness! Send a Cat Day greeting card, or Instagram video. Even if your cat ignores you when you take their picture, share it anyway. We all expect our cats to be both lovable and aloof at times. Either way, they're sure to capture your heart. If you just want to participate, rather than host your own National Cat Day Photo Contest you can find the official rules for one here: http://www.nationalcatday.com/contest.

You could take some home-baked cat cookies to your local cat shelter for the staff, or donate toys and blankets. And, just for kicks, paint your face, wear kitty ears, or dress in cat related fashion.

Colleen Paige, the founder of this Weird & Wacky Holiday says, "The goal of National Cat Day is to arrange the adoption of 10,000 shelter cats nationwide every Oct. 29." That's not a lofty goal, when you consider the United States population on January 1, 2016 was: 322,761,807.

According to Wikipedia, the day is supported by the American Society for the Prevention of Cruelty to Animals, a nonprofit organization which also works to encourage pet adoption.

I found several feline quotes & sayings that I have added to the appendix for your use on your National Cat Day cards and posts.

So, spread the love, and help bring an end to the cruelty. Oh, BTW, the official hashtag of the day is #nationalcatday!

Designed by Freepik

NOVEMBER

MONTH-LONG HOLIDAYS

Nov 19 Rabi'i: The Month of Migration (begins)
Nov 25 – Dec 3 Mexico: Guadalajara International Book Fair

American Diabetes Month, Aviation History Month, Banana Pudding Lovers Month, Diabetic Eye Disease Month, Lung Cancer Awareness Month, Movember, National Adoption Month, National Alzheimer's Disease Awareness Month, National Diabetes Month, National Epilepsy Awareness Month, National Family Caregivers Month, National Georgia Pecan Month, National Inspirational Role Models Month, National Long–Term Care Awareness Month, National Marrow Awareness Month, National Memoir Writing Month, National Native American Heritage Month, National Novel Writing Month, Peanut Butter Lovers Month, Picture Book Month, PPSI AIDS Awareness Month, Prematurity Awareness Month, Vegan Month, Worldwide Bereaved Siblings Month

WEEK-LONG HOLIDAYS

Nov 1 – 5 & 8 – 12 Edgar Allan Poe Evermore

Nov 1 – 7 National Patient Accessibility Week

Nov 3 – 5 Coin, Jewelry, & Stamp Expo: California (Pasadena), World Championship Punkin Chunkin (tentative)

Nov 6 – 10 National Young Reader's Week

Nov 8 – 11 International Dyslexia Association Reading, Literacy and Learning Conference (Atlanta, GA)

Nov 3 – 5 Coin, Jewelry, & Stamp Expo: America (Anaheim, CA)

Nov 10 – 12 National Donor Sabbath

Nov 13 – 17 American Education Week

Nov 13 – 19 National Book Awards Week

Nov 13 – 20 Miami Book Fair International

Nov 19 – 25 Better Conversation Week, Church/State Separation Week, National Family Week, National Game & Puzzle Week™

Nov 19 – 26 National Bible Week

DAILY HOLIDAYS

1. *All Hallows or All Saints Day, Antigua and Barbuda Independence Day, European Union (1993), Extra Mile Day, Hockey Mask Day, Mexico: Day of the Dead, *National Authors' Day, National Cook for Your Pets Day
2. *All Souls Day, *First Scheduled Radio Broadcast (1920), National Men Make Dinner Day, National Traffic Directors Day, *Plan Your Epitaph Day, United Nations: International Day to End Impunity for Crimes Against Journalists

3. *Cliché Day, Dewey Day, *Japan: Culture Day, Micronesia & Panama: Independence Day, National Medical Science Liaison Awareness and Appreciation Day, Public Television Day, *Sandwich Day, SOS Day

4. *King Tut Tomb Discovery (1922), Mischief Night, National Bison Day, *National Chicken Lady Day, National Easy Bake Oven Day, Pumpkin Destruction Day, Sadie Hawkins Day, Terlingua International Chili Championship, UNESCO Day, *Will Rogers (1879)

5. Daylight Saving Time Ends, *England: Guy Fawkes Day, *Roy Rogers (1911), *Shattered Backboard Day, United Nations: World Tsunami Awareness Day, Vivian Leigh–Scarlett O'Hara Day (1913), Zero Tasking Day

6. Fill Your Staplers Day, Job Action Day, Saxophone Day, *United Nations: International Day for Preventing the Exploitation of the Environment in War and Armed Conflict

7. Madam Curie Day, First Black Governor Elected (1989), General Election Day

8. Abet and Aid Punsters Day, Cook Something Bold and Pungent Day, Shakespeare Authorship Mystery Day, *X–ray Day

9. *Berlin Wall Opened (1989), Cambodia: Independence Day, East Coast Blackout (1965), Germany: Kristallnacht, National Child Safety Council Day, Return Day

10. *Area Code Day (1951), Claude Rains Day, Marine Corps Day, *Veterans Day (observed)

11. Angola: Independence Day, *Bonza Bottler Day™, Canada: Remembrance Day, Columbia: Cartagena Independence Day, Death/Duty Day, England: Remembrance Day, God Bless America Day, Japan: Origami Day, Martinmas, Poland: Independence Day, Sweden: Saint Martin's Day, Switzerland: Martinmas Goose (Martinigians), Veterans Day

12. Mexico: Postman's Day, World Pneumonia Day

13. Holland Tunnel Day, World Orphans Day

14. India: Children's Day, International Girls Day, Loosen Up Lighten Up Day, Moby Dick Day, Claude Monet Day, Spirit of NSA (National Speakers Association) Day, *United Nations: World Diabetes Day

15. *America Recycles Day, Belgium: Dynasty Day, Brazil: Republic Day, George Spelvin Day, Gypsy Condemnation Order Day (1943), Japan: Shichi–Go–San, *National Bundt (Pan) Day, National Educational Support Professionals Day

16. Estonia: Day of National Rebirth, France: Beaujolais Nouveau Release Day, Great American Smoke-out (third Thursday), *Lewis and Clark Expedition Reaches Pacific Ocean (1805), Saint Eustatius, West Indies: Statia and America Day, *United Nations: International Day for Tolerance, World Philosophy Day

17. *Homemade Bread Day, National Unfriend Day, Substitute Educators Day, Suez Canal Day, World Prematurity Day

18. International Games Day, Latvia: Independence Day, *Married to a Scorpio Support Day, *Mickey Mouse's Birthday (1928)

19. Alascattalo Day (About Alaska & humor), Belize: Garifuna Day, Cold War Ends (1990), *Dedication Day (1862), Gandhi Day, Garfield Day, Germany: Volkstrauertag, *"Have A Bad Day" Day, Puerto Rico: Discovery Day, United Nations: World Day of Remembrance for Road Traffic Victims

20. *Bill of Rights Day, Edwin Powell Hubble Day, *Mandelbrot Day (1924), Mexico: Revolution Day, *Name Your PC Day, Transgender Day of Remembrance, *United Nations: African Industrialization Day, United Nations: Universal Children's Day

21. *Sir Samuel Cunard (1787), *United Nations: World Television Day, World Hello Day

22. Charles De Gaulle Day 1890), *George Eliot (1819), Germany: Buss Und Bettag, Humane Society of the US Day (1954), Lebanon: Independence Day, Tie One On Day™, Thanksgiving Day, Turkey–free Thanksgiving Day

23. Billy the Kid Day, Boris Karloff Day, Family Day in Nevada, Fibonacci Day, Harpo Marx Day, Japan: Labor Thanksgiving Day

24. Black Friday, Brownielocks Day, Brunette Pride Day, Buy Nothing Day, *Celebrate Your Unique Talent Day, *Dale Carnegie (1888),*D.B. Cooper Day, National Flossing Day, Native American Heritage Day, Sinkie Day

25. *Andrew Carnegie (1835), International Aura Awareness Day, *JFK Day (1960), Saint Catherine's Day, Small Business Saturday, Suriname: Independence Day, United Nations: International Day For the Elimination of Violence Against Women Day

26. Charles Schultz (1922), *Eric Sevareid (1912), Germany: Totensonntag, Handel's Messiah Sing-Along

27. Bruce Lee Day, Cider Monday, Cyber Monday, Face Transplant Day, Switzerland: Zibelemarit (Onion Market)

28. *Albania: Independence Day (1912), Giving Tuesday, *Lévi–Strauss (1908), Mauritania: Independence Day, Panama: Independence from Spain

29. Alcott Day, *CS Lewis (1898), *Electronic Greetings Day, *United Nations: International Day of Solidarity With The Palestinian People

30. Barbados: Independence Day, *Computer Security Day, Saint Andrew's Day, *Stay Home Because You're Well Day

HOLIDAY MARKETING IDEAS FOR NOVEMBER

Movember — The aim of Movember is to raise awareness of men's health issues such as depression and different forms of cancer, because men's health is in crisis. Men are dying too young. It is a charity event and not just a reason to grow a mustache. Secondly, there are rules for Movember that should be followed, so be a good sport. So, as we look for ways to make this a Movember to remember consider a fundraising event for this worthy cause. Get involved. This isn't just a guy thing, it touches us all.

To make it fun, throughout the month, sport your mustache photos, even the gals can get involved. Check out the official website at: https://us.movember.com/ for ideas and tools to assist you in hosting your own successful event. When you do so, be sure to get the media behind you to raise even more for this worthy cause and, of course, to get your business noticed.

STOP MEN DYING TOO YOUNG
JOIN THE MOVEMENT FOR MEN'S HEALTH
MOVEMBER.COM

Nov 4 Mischief Night — This is the night that England, Australia, and New Zealand celebrate the failure of the plot to blow up the Houses of Parliament, with bonfires and firecrackers. With your sights set on plans gone awry, why not host your own Mischief Night gala. Show the world how to do things the right way, the way that will lead them to success, beginning with a solid plan, and follow through. Add some mischief to the mix and you're sure to have a dynamite event. You could even have a Grand Mischief Maker Award! You'll find a 3" square you can use to make your GMM Pin Award along with its counterpart Mischief Maker design, in the appendix.

On a much smaller scale you could have a backyard bar-b-que with fireworks afterwards. Or just share on social media tweets and helpful advice.

Nov 13 Holland Tunnel Day — Begun in 1920 and completed in 1927, the tunnel is named after Clifford Milburn Holland (1883 – 1924), Chief Engineer on the project, who died before it was completed. Tunnel designer Ole Singstad finished Holland's work. So, it has nothing to do with the county, nor is it located there. It is actually an underwater bridge linking Interstate 78 on the island of Manhattan in New York City, with I-78 and NJ 139 in Jersey City, New Jersey on the mainland of the United States. How's that for throwing you totally off track?

Nevertheless, being that we are talking about bridges, thoughts come to mind of relationship building, both business and personal. Guidance counselors, therapists, communication coaches, business building services, and any number of professional all could make good use of this Weird & Wacky Holiday to showcase their business.

If you can't think of anything to do or how your business, book, or service could benefit from building a marketing campaign around this holiday, you could always either partner with someone who does, or send out eCards to your customers, clients, and friends.

Manhattan entrance to Holland Tunnel, 1985

Nov 16 World Philosophy Day — Today is all about human thought and the development and sharing of ideas worldwide. It helps us to build and live better lives, treating each other and our environment in a more humane and ethical way.

Bronze figure of Kashmiri in Meditation by Malvina Hoffman Wellcome M0005215.jpg CC BY 4.0

Put some thought into how you can share your ideas and learn and grow from the thoughts and ideas of others around you. Sharing quotes and sayings is a good start, but if you want to make a genuine impact, you have to get out of your comfort zone and your computer chair and get others involved in the sharing of ideas. After all, it isn't sharing unless you have at least two people participating.

There are many critical issues facing us today. Everything from the very breath we breathe to managing our businesses while raising a family. There's sure to be something to talk about and learn today. At the very least you could hunt down some famous quotes, post them, and then discuss them with others.

Donate to the Philosophy Foundation (see appendix for link). Any money raised is put towards providing specialist teachers to schools that need it most, but can't afford it. The organization aims to support young people in higher education studying philosophy. Make sure not to forget to send out your press releases to promote your charity drive.

Or, merely tune in to the live webcast of the philosophical debates on UNESCO's website. It can be streamed in French or English at the UNESCO site. You'll find the link in the resources section of the appendix.

Nov 20 Name Your PC Day — Everything we own, we tend to name; our car, our boat, our bathrooms, well, you get the picture. So, why not name the one thing we use more than any other object in our lives; our computer! One fun way to market your services today might be to post a picture of yours on the web and have folks help you name it. Yes, a contest could be a fun way to celebrate this Weird & Wacky Holiday. BTW, I hear Big Mac is already taken. *wink*

You can even go into your computer settings and change your PC's name so it is official. If you don't know how to do that, maybe you need to have somebody join you on your favorite meet up spot and explain it to not only you, but to those who want to join your little Name Your PC Day party. It's an easy thing to do, really! Your party guests could even share stories of how they came to name the PC what they did.

Your unique computer name can be chosen by your favorite theme, or subject. For example, Your favorite group, food, color, comic book character, or super hero. You get the gist. Make it both fun and unique. You never know what files will carry it over in their metadata.

If you want to send out or post a Happy Name Your PC Day card with instructions on how to change it on your computer you can find a sample in the appendix.

Nov 29 Electronic Greetings Day — With this Weird & Wacky Holiday I am reminded how much easier life has become in my lifetime. There were no TVs, let alone computers, when I was born. But, today we have both, and have had them for some time now.

As we look to celebrate this Weird & Wacky Holiday, the name tells us exactly what we need to be doing. When you look in the appendix you will find a whole host of eCard services to choose from. My two favorites are BlueMountain and Send Out Cards. While BlueMountain is a true eCard service, Send Out Cards offers the convenience of eCards with physical card delivery. However, since this is eCard Greeting Day, you are sure to want to send out fully eCard greetings to all your customers, clients, and friends.

So send out your eCard Greetings. And then use #ElectronicGreetingsDay to post on social media and encourage all your customers and friends to do the same. I have designed a card you can brand for your own needs in the appendix to get you started.

DECEMBER

MONTH-LONG HOLIDAYS

Dec 14 – Jan 5, 2018 Christmas Bird Count
Dec 17 – Feb 4, 2018 Take a New Year's Resolution to Stop Smoking (TANYRSS)

Bingo's Birthday Month, Christmas New Orleans Style, A Colonial Christmas, National Impaired Driving Prevention Month, National Write a Business Plan Month, Safe Toys and Gifts Month, Worldwide Food Service Safety Month

WEEK-LONG HOLIDAYS

Dec 3 – 10 Clerc-Gallaudet Week

Dec 4 – 8 Cookie Exchange Week

Dec 4 – 8 National Older Driver Safety Awareness Week

Dec 10 – 17 Human Rights Week

Dec 13 – 20 Chanukah

Dec 14 – 28 Halcyon Days

Dec 17 – 23 Saturnalia

Dec 26 – Jan 1, 2017 Kwanzaa

DAILY HOLIDAYS

1. Antarctica Day, *Basketball Day, *Bifocals at the Monitor Liberation Day, *Civil Air Patrol Day, Day With(out) Art, National Sales Person's Day, Portugal: Independence Day, Rosa Parks Day, *United Nations: World AIDS Day

2. *Artificial Heart Transplant Day (1967), England: Walter Plinge Day, *Joseph Bell (1837), *Safety Razor Day, *Special Education Day, United Arab Emirates: Independence Day, *United Nations: International Day for the Abolition of Slavery Day

3. Advent Sunday, First Heart Transplant (1967), International Day of Persons with Disabilities, *United Nations: International Day of Persons with Disabilities

4. Mary Celeste Discovery Day, National Grange Day, Saint Barbara's Day, *Samuel Butler (1835)

5. *AFL–CIO Founded (1955), Austria: Krampuslauf, *Bathtub Party Day, "Irrational Exuberance" Day, Montgomery Bus Boycott Remembrance Day, *United Nations: International Volunteer Day for Economic & Social Development, United Nations: World Soil Day, *Walt Disney (1901)

6. *National Miners' Day, *National Pawnbrokers Day, *Saint Nicholas Day, Special Kids Day

7. Iran: Students Day, National Christmas Tree Lighting (tentative), *National Fire Safety Council Founding (1979), *National Pearl Harbor Remembrance Day, *United Nations: International Civil Aviation Day

8. *Eli Whitney (1765), Feast of Immaculate Conception, Intermediate-Range Nuclear Forces Treaty (INF) Signed (1987), NAFTA Day, Official Lost and Found Day, Soviet Union Dissolved (1991)

9. America's First Formal Cremation (1792), Gingerbread Decorating Day, National Day of the Horse, *United Nations: International Anti-Corruption Day

10. *Ada Lovelace (1815), *Dewey Decimal System Day, *Emily Dickinson (1830), *Human Rights Day, James Addams Day, *Nobel Prize Day, *Thomas Hopkins Gallaudet (1787), *United Nations: Human Rights Day

11. *UNICEF Birthday, *United Nations: International Mountain Day

12. *Bonza Bottler Day™, Chanukah (begins at sundown), Day of Our Lady of Guadalupe, Kenya: Jamhuri Day (Independence Day), Mexico: Guadalupe Day, *Poinsettia Day, *Puerto Rico: Las Mañanitas

13. *New Zealand Discovery (1642), Sweden: Saint Lucia Day

14. *Doolittle Day, Nostradamus (1503), South Pole Discovery (1911)

15. *Bill of Rights Day, *Cat Herders Day, Puerto Rico: Navidades, Underdog Day

16. Bahrain: Independence Day, *Barbie and Barney Backlash Day, Boston Tea Party Day, *Jane Austen (1775), *Ludwig Van Beethoven (1770), Mexico: Posadas, *United Nations: Zionism Day

17. *Azteck Calendar Stone Discovery Day (1790), *Clean Air Day, *Joseph Henry (1797), *Wright Brothers Day

18. *Benjamin O Davis, Jr. (1912), *Joseph Grimaldi (1778), Mexico: Feast of Our Lady of Solitude, *Antonio Stradivari Death (1737), *United Nations: International Migrants Day

19. Titanic Day

20. Cathode-Ray Tube Day, *Mudd Day, *United Nations: International Human Solidarity Day

21. Celebrate Short Fiction Day, Benjamin Disraeli Birth (1804), *Crossword Puzzle Day, *Forefathers Day, *Heinrich Böll (1917),*Humbug Day, *Phileas Fogg Win A Wager Day, Pilgrim Landing, Yalda, Yule

22. Be a Lover of Silence Day, First Gorilla Born in Captivity (1956), *Giacomo Puccini (1858), Oglethorpe Day

23. *Federal Reserve System (1913), First Non-stop Flight Around the World (1987), HumanLight Celebration Day, Japan: Birthday of the Emperor, Metric Conversion Act (1975), Mexico: Feast of Radishes, *Transistor Day (1947)

24. *Christmas Eve , *James Prescott Joule (1818), Libya: Independence Day

25. *A'Phabet Day or No-L-Day, *Christmas Day, Cuba: Christmas Returns, *Clara Barton (1821), *Evangeline Cory Booth (1865), Washington Crosses the Delaware (1776)

26. *Bahamas: Junkanoo, Boxing Day, Ireland: Day of the Wren, Luxembourg: Blessing of the Wine, *Mao Tse-Tung (1893), *National Whiner's Day, Radium Day, Saint Stephen's Day, Second Day of Christmas, Slovenia: Independence Day, South Africa: Day of Goodwill, *United Nations: Boxing Day

27. *Johannes Kepler (1571), *Louis Pasteur (1822), Saint John

28. Asarah B'tevet, Australia: Proclamation Day, *Cinema Day, Endangered Species Day, *Holy Innocents Day or Childermas, *Pledge of Allegiance Day

29. Andrew Johnson Wreath-Laying, No Interruptions Day, Saint Thomas of Canterbury: Feast Day, *Tick Tock Day, *YMCA Day

30. *Falling Needles Family Fest Day, *Rudyard Kipling (1865), USSR DAY (1922)

31. *First Nights, First US Bank Opens (1781), *Japan: Namahage, *Leap Second Adjustment Time Day, *Make Up Your Mind Day, *New Year's Eve, New Year's Banished Words List, Saint Sylvester's Day, Scotland: Hogmany, *World Peace Meditation Day

HOLIDAY MARKETING IDEAS FOR DECEMBER

Bingo's Birthday Month — The game of Bingo was first manufactured in December 1929 by Edwin S. Lowe. Thus, we celebrate its humble beginnings in the month of December. Why not have your own Bingo Party on-line this month? Your guests can sign up to get the daily word that is on your branded game card which is filled with words pertaining to one subject matter, your business or career, or just random words. They have to opt in to play and you can build your customer list by adding them to your auto-responder. The first one to reach BINGO will win a prize donated by your game's sponsor, or something simple like a gift certificate. You'll find a sample to get you started in the appendix.

After coming up with this idea I found several others who have done this already. And, one of my on-line friends actually did this one year and had over 101 participants from the U.S., Canada, Iceland, France, Portugal, Italy, Ireland, Switzerland, Netherlands, and England.

NURSE BINGO™

CAN'T FIND MY PEN	SIMULTANEOUS CODES	EMPTY LINEN CART	CAUGHT WRONG MEDS	QUESTIONED ORDER
NPO PATIENT EATS	PATIENT = DRUG SEEKER	CHANGE OF SHIFT ADMISSION	PROJECTILE VOMIT	PATIENT LEFT AMA
PATIENT 'NEEDS' PRIVATE ROOM	IV WON'T STOP BEEPING	FREE SPACE	CAN'T FIND PATIENT	SNORING PATIENT WAKES FLOOR
PATIENT ON CELL PHONE	PATIENT CHART MISSING	PATIENT HAS 6+ VISITORS	VISITOR SAYS "MOM NEEDS HELP!"	SUSPECTED SWINE FLU
DECLINES MUCH NEEDED SHOWER	FAMILY MEMBER c/o DOCTOR	NAKED PATIENT IN HALL	CODE BROWN!	2 NURSES CALL IN

© JOURNAL OF NURSING JOCULARITY 2009. ALL RIGHTS RESERVED (YEP, ALL OF 'EM).

Dec 1 Antarctica Day — Today celebrates the International Treaty signed by 12 nations in Antarctica. Thus the theme is international cooperation. The official website, Our Spaces, link can be found in the resources section of this book. They have several suggestions and kits to use to help you plan your event or just listen in on their webinar.

An interesting fact is that Antarctica has no government! Therefore, it can only be used for peaceful purposes. No government, means no flag! So, creating Antarctica Flags of your own is a popular activity for today. But, for your business you might consider hosting or participating in a global mastermind group. You could meet up on Skype, or Google Hangouts, have a webinar, or create a Facebook Group. Getting other's input on issues you are facing in your life and business may be just what you or your attendees need today.

Dec 5 "Irrational Exuberance" Day — The term "irrational exuberance" derives from some words that Alan Greenspan, then chairman of the Federal Reserve Board in Washington, used in a black-tie dinner speech entitled " The Challenge of Central Banking in a Democratic Society". Today it is often used to describe a heightened state of speculative fervor.

Do I hear you say, "PARTY!!!?" Excuse my exuberance with the caps and extra exclamation marks. I just couldn't help myself. *wink* Get your excitement level pumped up and show some joy and happiness with those around you, for no other reason than to celebrate this Weird & Wacky Holiday.

Dec 11 United Nations: International Mountain Day — If you have a hard time figuring out how to promote your business using this Weird & Wacky Holiday, you aren't thinking hard enough. Open your mind to the possibilities before you to scale new heights in your business and you have a reachable goal. Call your gathering a 'Summit' just for the fun of it.

Whether your goal is to share about business, personal, or environmental issues, you are sure to find others who will take the climb with you and plant the flag of success at the peak of whichever mountain you decide to scale. Remember, there are no shortcuts to the top! Progress is made one step at a time. So, begin your planning in plenty of time to gather your team and attendees.

You can find an event flier template created just for this Weird & Wacky Holiday for you to use and customize to your needs. If you need help doing so, just email me at support@holiday-marketingguide.com.

Dec 20 Cathode-Ray Tube Day — Did you know that without the CRT we would never have seen our first television show? Yes, the Cathode-Ray Tube, better known as CRT is the science behind a few inventions, including the X-ray, and yes, even your computer screen. So, today we celebrate CRT Day to honor the benefit and influence it has had on our daily lives. I'd say that's a pretty big deal, wouldn't you?

So, lest we fail to see the light, tweet the day away with facts and photos about this important discovery. Other things you could do could include cards and eCards in celebration of this Weird & Wacky Holiday.

Dec 29 Tick Tock Day — Tick Tock Day is a reminder that there are only two, yes 2 days remaining in the year. Do you have any unfinished business that needs to be done in this calendar year? Not to put any pressure on you, I'm just sayin' . . .

If you have unfinished business, or need to cram one last thing into your remaining days this year, now's the time to do so. Did you have a New Year's Day resolution that you still haven't accomplished? You'd better get to it, 'cuz time is ticking away.

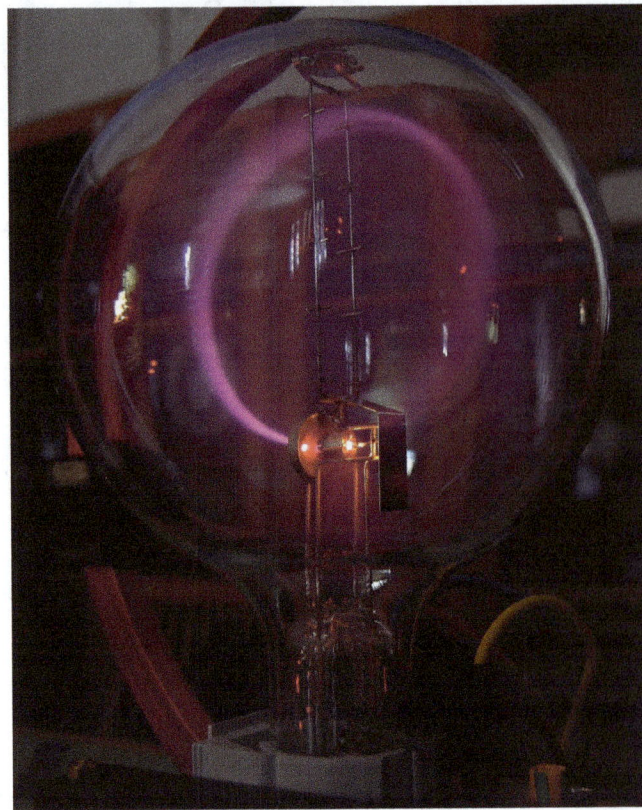

A beam of cathode rays in a vacuum tube bent into a circle by a magnetic field generated by a Helmholtz coil. Cathode rays are normally invisible; in this tube enough residual gas has been left that the gas atoms glow from fluorescence when struck by the fast moving electrons. Cyclotron motion smaller view CC BY-SA 3.0

#TickTockDay is the hashtag to post on social media today, if you were wondering.

Appendix A: SAMPLES

Sample Press Release

FOR IMMEDIATE RELEASE

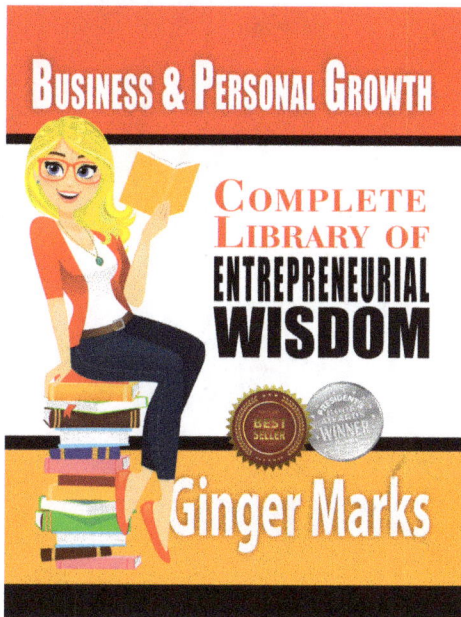

30+ YEAR LOCAL VETERAN BUSINESS OWNER / AUTHOR PARTNERS WITH PNC BANK

CLEARWATER, FL— SEPTEMBER 21, 2014 Local author and publisher, Ginger Marks, partners with Clearwater's PNC Bank to provide insight and advice for prospective, new, and experienced business owners. Ginger will be available to chat and sign copies of her award winning book, Complete Library of Entrepreneurial Wisdom, and PNC Financial experts will be on hand to field your questions and educate you on business financial matters.

Mrs. Marks has spent 30+ years in the Tampa Bay area honing her skill as an entrepreneur. Having owned and operated multiple businesses, including a restaurant and a multimillion dollar surgical clinic, she knows her way around business and how to operate one successfully.

Mrs. Marks states, "Owning a business takes many talents and the determination to succeed. In the course of my business operations I have experienced both the ups and the downs of the financial market. Without the knowledge of how to structure your finances to support your dreams you endanger your success. This is why I have partnered with PNC with the release of this important work."

Event date and location: October 9, 2014 between 5:30 and 6:30 pm at 2498 Gulf-to-Bay Blvd. Books available at your local bookstore and at this event.

# # #

MEDIA CONTACT: Ginger Marks, ginger.marks@documeantdesings.com 1 – 727 – 565 – 8500.

Rising Star Sticker

Design by DocUmeant Designs

Customize these designs with your business name and URL. Need help? Contact Ginger for assistance.

Worldwide Rising Star Pin

Design by DocUmeant Designs
This can be colored to match your brand if you like.

Skeleton Bone Pretzels

Ingredients:

25 Pretzel sticks
1/2 to 1 cup White Chocolate chips (melted)
Mini-Marshmallows

Directions:

Take a pretzel stick and put a mini marshmallow on each end.

Melt white chocolate chips in a microwave on 50% power. Stir every 30 seconds. To keep it from hardening too fast you can add a drop or two of oil. Stir well.

Dip pretzels with marshmallows on ends in white chocolate and then put it on wax or parchment paper and let it set. You can also stick them in the fridge.

Even the kids will enjoy helping to make these!

To add to the mix try whipping up a few Jell-O eyeballs: recipe and directions are here: https://www.youtube.com/watch?v=xOGZdTHSSGU

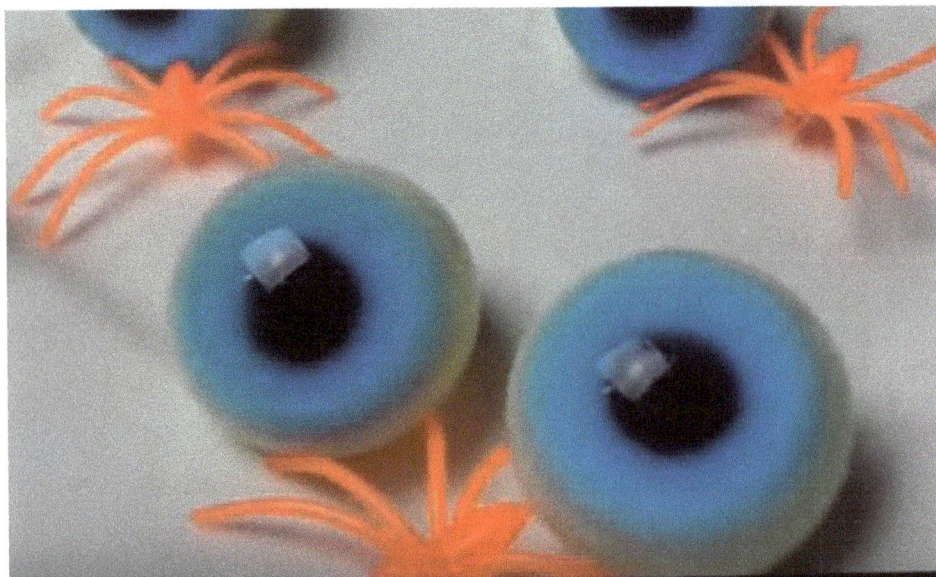

Happy Beer Can Appreciation Day Cards

Designed by DocUmeantDesigns.com

DocUmeantDesigns.com wishes you a

HAPPY BEER CAN APPRECIATION DAY

Happy Beer Can Appreciation Day

Success comes in **CANS** *not* **CAN'TS**

www.DocUmeantPublishing.com

Relationship Bill of Rights

Words courtesy of Loveisrespect.org

National Teen Dating Violence Awareness and Prevention Month, Feb 2017

- You have rights in your relationship. Everyone does, and those rights can help you set boundaries that should be respected by both partners in a healthy relationship.

- You have the right to privacy, both on-line and off

- You have the right to feel safe and respected

- You have the right to decide who you want to date or not date

- You have the right to say no at any time (to sex, to drugs or alcohol, to a relationship), even if you've said yes before

- You have the right to hang out with your friends and family and do things you enjoy, without your partner getting jealous or controlling

- You have the right to end a relationship that isn't right or healthy for you

- You have the right to live free fromviolence and abuse

Courtesy of DocUmeant Publishing & Desgins
www.DocUmeantPublishing.com • www.DocUmeantDesigns.com

Teen Dating Violence Awareness Flier

Designed by DocUmeantDesigns.com

Bubble Gum Wrapper templates

Pick up the gum at a dollar store; they come in a package of four for $1. The covers are printed on standard printer paper and print 6 per sheet.

What you'll need:

Small packages of gum from your local dollar store
Gum wrapper Printable
Tape
Card, if desired
Scissors or paper trimmer

Directions:

Cut out and wrap the gum with the cover. Fold over the edges and secure with tape. If desired print a card with your message and brand it with your company logo and contact information. Secure wrapped gum to card with two sided tape. Share with everyone you know.

Alternately you can print small tags rather than the cards. Using a hole punch place a hole near one end and attach with string or ribbon.

Gum Wrapper Templates

Stick Gum Wrapper

BUBBLE GUM DAY
February 3, 2017
[Your business brand here]

Square Gum Wrapper

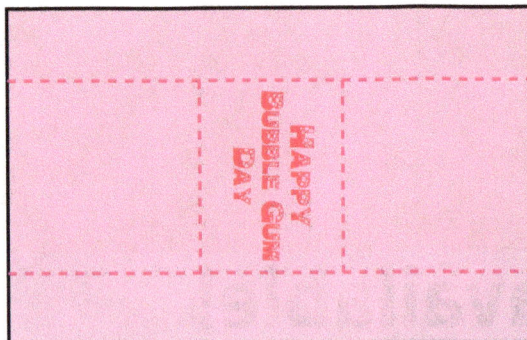

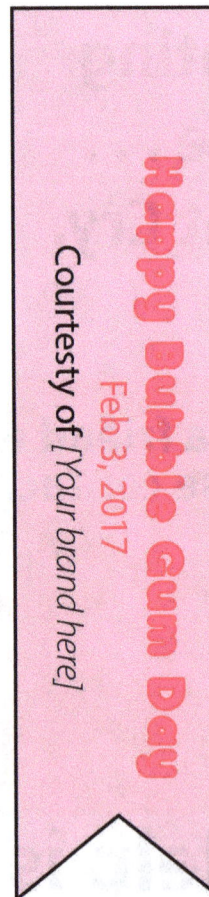

HAPPY BUBBLE GUM DAY

Happy Bubble Gum Day
Feb 3, 2017
Courtesty of [Your brand here]

Bubble Contest

Courtesy of http://pagingsupermom.com/2013/04/measuring-bubbles-gum-contest/

Materials:

One brands of bubble gum to keep it fair (Dubble Bubble, Bubblicious, Bubble Yum, Bazooka, Big League Chew, etc.)
Ruler & 2 Paper Clip or Bubble Meter
Timer
Paper & pen for recording measurements
Contestants

Procedures:

Each person chews that same brand of gum for 10 minutes.
Begin blowing bubbles with one piece of gum.
Measure each bubble using the ruler and paper clip. This will give you the bubble diameter in centimeters.
Write down the diameter of each bubble next to the contestant's name.

Ruler & 2 Paper Clips Method
Put one paper clip on the ruler at zero. Use the other to measure the size of the bubble.

Bubble Gum Contest Measuring Tool

Designed by DocUmeantDesigns.com

INSTRUCTIONS: Enlarge and print this template onto heavy card stock.* Carefully cut out both sides following the black outline to create your Bubble Meter. Punch a small hole where indicated by the silver circle, and attach the two sides together using a metal brad. Designate a person to judge the contestant's bubbles using the assembled Bubble Meter.

During the contest, the judge should quickly fit the tool's ends to either side of the first contestant's bubble, and hold the meter's measurement to compare to subsequent bubbles. Enlarge the meter's measurement gap as necessary when a new, larger bubbles emerge. The Bubble Champion is the person whose measured bubble is the largest when the contest time period is over.

*If you would like the full-size template contact me and I'll be happy to provide it to you at no cost for you to brand to your business.

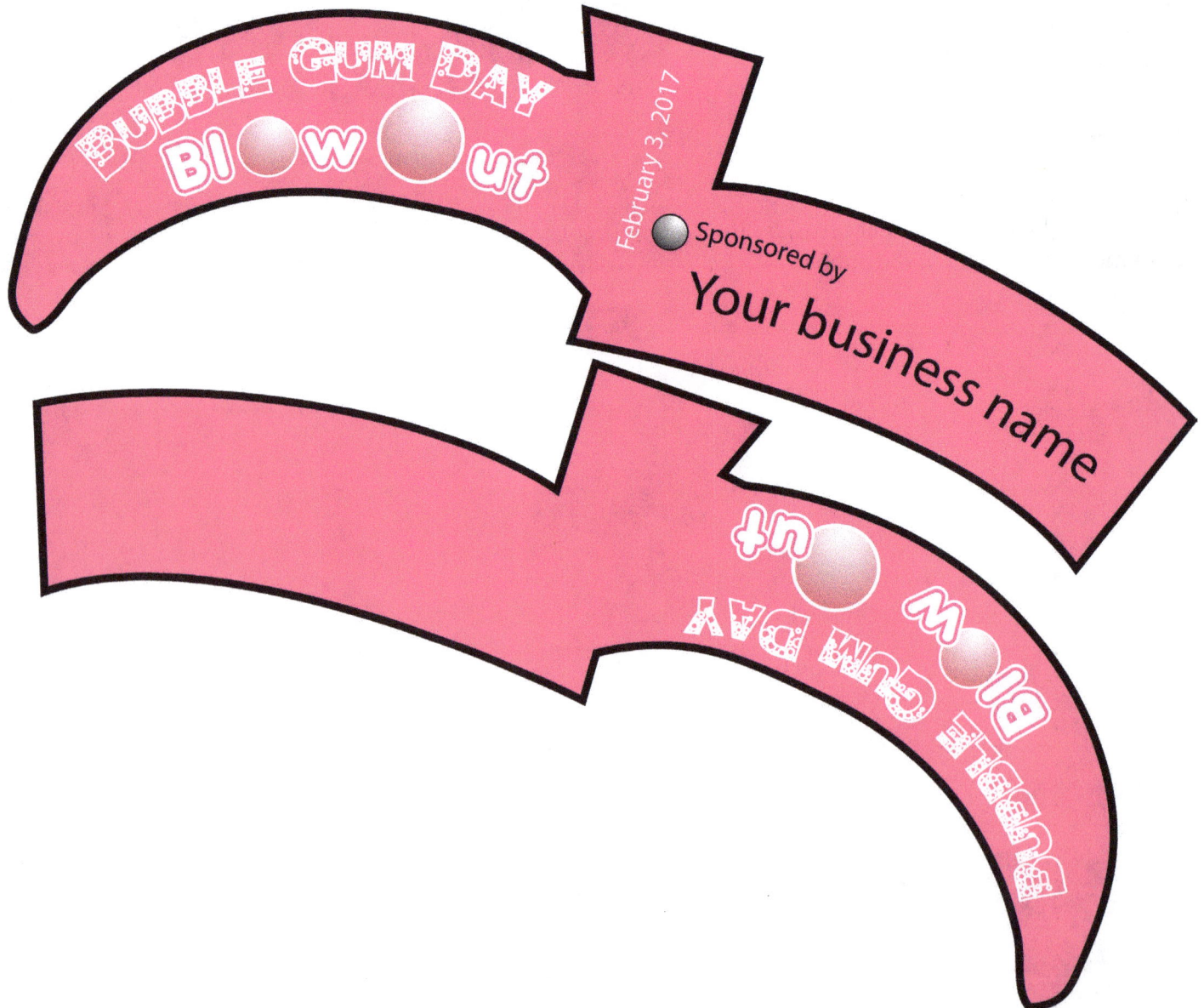

Guitar Note Card

Design by DocUmeantDesigns.com

This image has a 9 pt bleed for full coverage on your card stock. To make this note card simply purchase 3-1/2 x 4-7/8 inch blank note card stationary and print the design on the cover. To make your cards extra-special you can use old sheet music to line the inside of your envelopes.

If you need help getting these created send me a quick email and I'll be happy to assist you.

Interstate Highway Sign

Courtesy of Wikimedia

Print on card stock. Put your message on the back. Don't forget to add your business brand.

Business Loop Sign

Courtesy of Wikimedia

Print on card stock. Put your message on the back. Don't forget to add your business brand.

Learn What Your Name Means Day Card

Designed by DocUmeantDesigns.com

Use this design as either a one or two-sided card. Print with no text on it or contact Ginger for custom designs.

DESIGNED BY DOCUMEANTDESIGNS.COM

HEIDI

Means

NOBILITY

Learn What Your Name Means Day Envelope

Designed by DocUmeantDesigns.com

Use this as your envelope to make your message special.

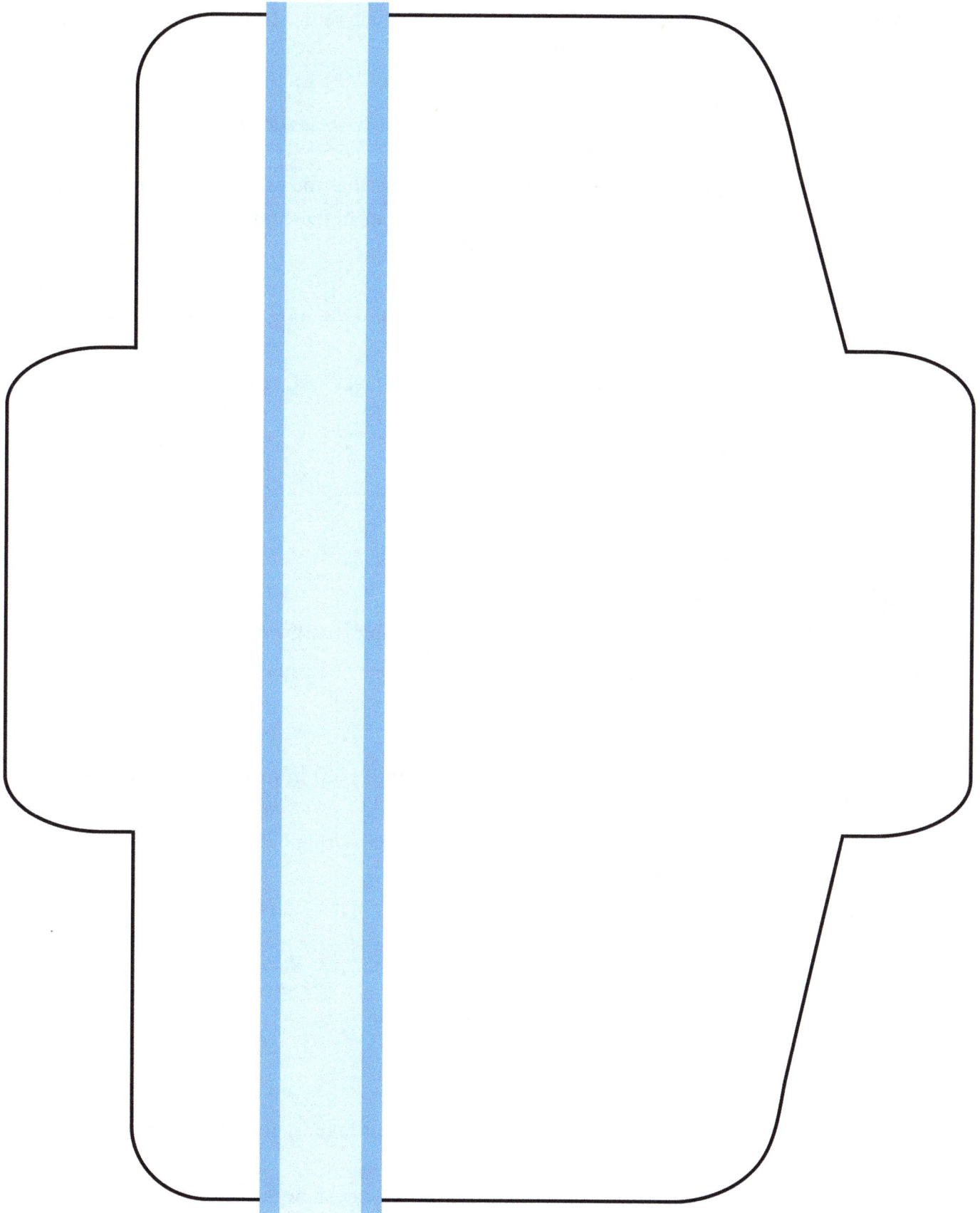

Weekly Twitter Hashtag Guide

The following is a short list of Twitter hashtags. Use them at your own risk of getting popular and social on Twitter Day and beyond. This is just the beginning. You can search Twitter for appropriate hashtags for your business or create your own. #Free and #Giveaway are two that get a whole lot of attention, but the list goes on and on. In the appendix resources section you will find a Twitter Hashtag source link. Use it as your own peril! You just might get addicted to Twitter and/or #hashtagmania!

3 Quick Tips for Using This Tactic:

1. Do your research. Hashtag meanings change over time. And some hashtags don't mean what you think they mean.
2. For Instagram, keep a note on your phone with groups of hashtags that you can cut and paste quickly.
3. You don't always have to produce the content yourself to participate in these fun hashtags. Search the hashtag, find a post you like, and retweet it, share it or re-gram it.

Monday

#MCM or #ManCrushMonday – great for lighthearted and humorous brands, this hashtag is used with photos good-looking celebrities

#MusicMonday – if you're in the entertainment industry, this is a great hashtag to introduce new artists or old favorites

#MountainMonday – photos of mountains

#MeowMonday – for all things feline! Post pictures of cats, retweet adoptable cats, or recommend Twitter accounts with good cat information.

#ManicMonday (your crazy post-weekend work/school schedule)

#ManicureMonday – no, not your lawn, those beautiful digits!

#MondayBlues – just the complete opposite, sympathize with people over how horrible Monday is

#MotivationMonday or #MondayMotivation – perfect for almost any industry, use this to share inspirational quotes to start the week off

Tuesday

#TipTuesday – great for any business, this is your chance to be the expert in your industry and share your knowledge and advice

#TT or #TransformationTuesday – this hashtag is accompanied with a split before and after photo, great for showing progress over time

#TravelTuesday – it may be a little limited for most companies, but if it relates to you, hashtag fun and exciting places to visit

#TuesdayBoozeDay – it's about celebrations and of course booze

#TuesdayTreat – use this to offer something special to your audience

Wednesday

#WineWednesday – wine lovers, tips, tastes, and tools

#WellnessWednesday – a little more restrictive to health and fitness brands, use this to share great foods or exercises

#WomanCrushWednesday – the counterpart for Man Crush Monday, show those beautiful ladies you're in love with

#HumpDay – we all know what this is. Use it to either complain about the difficulties of the week to empathize with your audience, or share something motivational to help people push through.

#WisdomWednesday or #WednesdayWisdom – similar to Motivation Monday, use this to share words of wisdom

#Women2Follow – women whom you recommend to follow

#WayBackWednesday – any company can use this hashtag to show old photos of their early years

#WaterfallWednesday – photos of waterfalls around the world

#HealthyHumpDay – healthy lifestyle choices, tips and recipes, too.

#WoofWednesday – all that's cute and cuddly in the puppy or dog world

#WonderfulWednesday – this one is for sharing happy moments, heartwarming pictures, and warm wishes.

Thursday

#TBT or #ThrowbackThursday – similar to Way Back Wednesday but more popular, share those old photos

#ThirstyThursday (drinking on Thursday) – talk about drinking, whether it's healthy drinks or alcohol

#Thursdate – for midweek dates

#ThursdayFunDay – similar to Monday Funday, show pics of your staff having fun, or it can be more open to sharing anything fun

#ThankfulThursday – good for reflecting on things to be thankful for

Friday

#FF or #FollowFriday – use it to tag and highlight other people or brands worth following, it's great for making connections

#FBF or #FlashbackFriday – similar to Throwback Thursday but not as popular, it follows the same theme of sharing old pics

#FridayFact or #FactFriday – share something funny or alternatively, someone at your practice having a good time

#FridayFunday or #FridayFun – similar to Monday Funday, show pics of your staff having fun, or it can be more open to sharing anything fun

#FridayReads – books, books, and more books

#Friday or #FridayNight – as we ease into the weekend, this hashtag can be used for asking about weekend plans or sharing them

Saturday

#Caturday – it's true – Saturdays are all about cats on Twitter

#SaturdaySwag or #SaturdayShenanigans (for shopping) – perfect for clothing brands, but can be used for other products as well, show great lifestyle pics

#SaturdayNight – similar to Friday night, share or poll your ongoing weekend activities

#SocialSaturday – this is probably the most open hashtag of them all, use it to share anything that's fun and amusing

Sunday

#SS or #SelfieSunday – get personal with this hashtag by having you and your staff take selfies, or show pics of your office

#Catbox Sunday – photos of cats in boxes. 'Nuff said!

#SundayFunday – same as Monday Funday, share what you're up to on a Sunday afternoon, or suggest an activity for your audience

#LazySunday – for your lazy Sunday activities with your furry friends

#SameSexSunday – for recommending people in the LGBT community

Quirky Country Music Song Titles

1. Tequila Makes Her Clothes Fall Off—Joe Nichols
2. You Look Like I Need a Drink—Justin Moore
3. My Give a Damn's Busted—Jo Dee Messina
4. Save a Horse, Ride a Cowboy—Big & Rich
5. Did I Shave My Legs for This?—Deana Carter
6. Being Drunk's a Lot like Loving You—Kenny Chesney
7. All My Exes Live in Texas—George Strait
8. Man! I Feel Like a Woman—Shania Twain
9. Fax Me a Beer—Hank Williams Jr.
10. I'm So Lonesome I Could Cry—Hank Williams
11. You Can't Rollerskate in a Buffalo Herd—Roger Miller
12. I've Got Tears in My Ears From Lying on My Back Crying Over You—Homer & Jethro
13. May the Bird of Paradise Fly Up Your Nose—Little Jimmy Dickens
14. She Made Toothpicks Out of the Timber of My Heart—Homer and Jethro
15. She Thinks My Tractor's Sexy— Kenny Chesney
16. Honky Tonk Badonkadonk—Trace Adkins
17. How Come Your Dog Don't Bite Nobody But Me—Webb Pierce & Mel Tillis
18. Flushed From the Bathroom of Your Heart—Johnny Cash
19. I Keep Forgettin' That I Forgot About You—Wynn Stewart
20. Here's a Quarter (Call Someone Who Cares)—Travis Tritt

Quirky Country Music Song Titles Contests

1. Name the artist who sang the song (see previous page)
2. Give a line from the song and ask for the title (see next page)
3. Name that tune: Play a small part of the music and have the contestants name the tune
4. Post YouTube videos of your contestants singing a Quirky Country Music Song (category winners or allow multiple winners)

Quirky Country Song Music Lyrics

Tequila Makes Her Clothes Fall Off
"She can handle any champagne brunch / A bridal shower with Bacardi punch / Jell-O shooters full of Smirnoff / But tequila makes her clothes fall off / She'll start by kicking out of her shoes / Lose an earring in her drink / Leave her jacket in the bathroom stall / Drop a contact down the sink / She don't mean nothing, she's just havin' fun / Tomorrow she'll say, 'Oh, what have I done?' / Her friends will joke about the stuff she lost / Yeah, tequila makes her clothes fall off."

Did I Shave My Legs For This?
"I bought these new heels, did my nails / Had my hair done just right / I thought this new dress was a sure bet / For romance tonight / Well, it's perfectly clear, between the TV and beer / I won't get so much as a kiss / As I head for the door, I turn around to be sure / Did I shave my legs for this?"

Fax Me a Beer
"I got a brand new VCR, it's got 29, 000 functions / And I can't make the damn thing work, so there goes Petticoat Junction / That's when I got the best idea I think I had in years / I think I'll be cool and invent the tool that'll fax me a beer / Would you like me to fax me a beer? / This invention is gonna set the whole world on its ear / The old office code will never be the same / When it comes out cold and clear / Sit back, relax, and punch ol' fax and I'll fax you a beer / Sit back and drank and give thanks to Hank and I'll fax you a beer."

You Can't Rollerskate in a Buffalo Herd
"You can't rollerskate in a buffalo herd / But you can be happy if you've a mind to / You can't take a shower in a parakeet cage / But you can be happy if you've a mind to."

I've Got Tears in My Ears From Lying on My Back Crying Over You
"Since the day I found you were untrue / And if I don't get up pretty soon I'll turn into a sleepy lagoon / I've got tears in my ears from lyin' on my back / In my bed while I cry over you."

May the Bird of Paradise Fly Up Your Nose
"May the bird of paradise fly up your nose / May an elephant caress you with his toes / May your wife be plagued with runners in her hose / May the bird of paradise fly up your nose."

She Made Toothpicks Out of the Timber of My Heart
"Like a buzzsaw rips a pole, she made sawdust of my soul / She made toothpicks of the timber of my heart / When she rolled me down that hill and she run me through the mill / She made toothpicks of the timber of my heart."

She Thinks My Tractor's Sexy
"She thinks my tractor's sexy / It really turns her on / She's always starin' at me / While I'm chuggin' along / She likes the way it's pullin' while we're tillin' up the land / She's even kind of crazy 'bout my farmer's tan / She's the only one who really understands what gets me / She thinks my tractor's sexy."

Honky Tonk Badonkadonk
"Shut my mouth, slap your grandma / There outta be a law / Get the sheriff on the phone / Lord have mercy, how's she even get them britches on / That honky tonk badonkadonk"

How Come Your Dog Don't Bite Nobody But Me
"How come your dog don't bite nobody but me? / Well, he never bites the postman, he licks the milkman's hand / But every time I come around he thinks I'm the booger man."

Flushed From the Bathroom of Your Heart

"And now you say, "You've got me out of your conscience" / I've been flushed from the bathroom of your heart / In the garbage disposal of your dreams, I've been ground up, dear / On the river of your plans, I'm up the creek / Up the elevator of your future, Ive been shafted / On the calendar of your events, I'm last week."

I Keep Forgettin' That I Forgot About You

"I keep forgettin' not to remember you to get you out of my mind / Never more to be swayin' by all of your charms / I keep forgettin' not to remember you oh so much of the time / How I wish you had stayed here in my arms / There's no sleep for me no more / I stay awake and walk the floor / I keep forgettin' that we're supposed to be true / Loneliness is my downfall for some time / I almost climb the wall / I keep forgettin' that I've forgot about you."

Here's a Quarter (Call Someone Who Cares)

"Call someone who'll listen and might give a damn / Maybe one of your sordid affairs / But don't you come 'round here handin' me none of your lines / Here's a quarter, call someone who cares."

Who's Gonna Mow Your Grass

"Who's gonna bring you your breakfast in bed? / Who's gonna whisper, goodnight? / Who's gonna keep you as warm as toast / On those cold winter nights? / And who's gonna be your puppy dog / When I'm a thing of the past? / Hey, who's gonna mow your grass?"

Cowboy Themed Cupcakes

Use your favorite cupcake recipe and frosting.

You will need

Frosted cupcakes

Chocolate potato chips

Rollo candy

String licorice

Directions

After frosting your cupcakes top with the following, in order.

Chocolate dipped potato chip

Chocolate Rollo candy wrapped with red string licorice (or your favorite flavor)

Enjoy.

How to Hug Your Local Medievalist

A Helpful Table for the Uninformed

Courtesy of Natalie Grinnell (http://funnierthangrading.blogspot.com/)

You are a:	May you hug your local medievalist?	How?	Exceptions:
Family member	Damned right!	With love and affection	You owe your local medievalist money
Close friend	Not only may, but must	Briefly, but fully	You have not bathed today
Casual friend	You may	While making an awkward joke	You have issues
Fellow medievalist	Enthusiastically!	While making a joke in an archaic language	You are an art historian
Student	Only if you are completely comfortable doing so (and not drunk)	Virtual hug preferred; side-hug, Duggar-style, may be acceptable	You cannot spell medievalist
Colleague	You may	In public, so that no one gets the wrong idea	You are that creepy guy
Dean, provost or others of that ilk	Only with care, discretion and fake cheerfulness	Side-hug, preferably while holding a mug of coffee	You are about to assign the medievalist to the Committee from Hell
Former student	There's no law against it	Virtually	You gave him/her a bad rating on the Site That Shall Not Be Named
Beowulf	If your uncle's father was an ally to the medievalist's grandfather…yes	Gently	You sometimes forget to let go of other people's body parts
Cat	You may. But you won't.	With claws in and a long-suffering look	You are a cat.

Fun Facts about Ferrets

Designed by DocUmeantDesigns.com

Contact Ginger for the full size image or to customize it with your brand

Fun Facts about Ferrets

- Ferrets have been domesticated pets dating back as far as BC 450
- hey are related to Europeon polecats When threatened they dance
- Black-footed ferrets are on the endangered species list
- Adult males are called Hobs; females are Jills and their offspring are called Business
- They are used to hunt rabbits
- Ferrets helped lay wire for the millennium concert in London
- Have been known to attack human babies
- Females can die if they go too long without mating

Happy National Ferret Day
April 2, 2017

Provided to you by DocUmeantDesigns.com

85

Pin the Tail on the Beaver

Design by DocUmeantDesigns.com

Full size pattern available. Contact Ginger for your free copy. Not for resale.

Happy Muffin Day Card

Designed by DocUmeantDesigns.com

Brand this card with your business name. Print it on a 4- by 6-inch card and be sure to write a favorite recipe on the back to ensure retention by the recipient.

You'll find a few recipes that you are sure to enjoy on the following pages courtesy of DamnDelicious.com.

Blueberry Muffins with Blueberry Jam

The best blueberry muffins ever with homemade blueberry jam swirled right into the batter!

YIELD: 12 minutes
PREP TIME: 15 minutes; COOK TIME: 25 minutes
TOTAL TIME: 40 minutes

Ingredients

2 cups blueberries, divided

3/4 cup and 1 tablespoon sugar, divided

2 cups all-purpose flour

1 teaspoon cinnamon

2 teaspoons baking powder

1/2 teaspoon salt

2/3 cup buttermilk

1/4 cup (1/2 stick) unsalted butter, melted

1/4 cup vegetable oil

2 large eggs

1 teaspoon vanilla extract

FOR THE LEMON SUGAR TOPPING

1/4 cup sugar

Zest of 1 lemon

Directions

Preheat oven to 400 degrees F. Line a 12-cup standard muffin tin with paper liners or coat with nonstick spray; set aside.

In a medium saucepan, combine 1 cup blueberries and 1 tablespoon sugar. Bring to a boil; reduce heat and simmer, stirring occasionally, until sauce has thickened, about 5 minutes. Let cool 10-15 minutes.

To make the lemon sugar topping, combine sugar and lemon zest, rubbing the zest into the sugar with your fingertips; set aside.

In a large bowl, combine flour, remaining 3/4 cup sugar, cinnamon, baking powder and salt.

In a large glass measuring cup or another bowl, whisk together buttermilk, butter, vegetable oil, eggs and vanilla. Pour mixture over dry ingredients and stir using a rubber spatula just until moist. Add remaining 1 cup blueberries and gently toss to combine.

Scoop the batter evenly into the muffin tray. Top each muffin with 1 teaspoon blueberry jam, swirling into the batter using figure eight motions. Sprinkle with lemon sugar mixture.

Place into oven and bake for 15-17 minutes, or until a tester inserted in the center comes out clean.

Remove from oven and cool on a wire rack.

Adapted from The Little Kitchen.
This delicious recipe brought to you by DAMN DELICIOUS http://damndelicious.net/2012/08/13/muffinmonday-blueberry-muffins-with-blueberry-jam/

Chocolate, Hazelnut and Olive Oil Muffins

These are some of the nicest gluten-free muffins I've ever made/eaten. They are slightly more crumbly than their gluten-filled siblings due to the rice flour but not really so much that you'd notice. I love these warmed up a little so that the chocolate chips are all melted, but they're equally good cold. They should last a couple of days in the fridge although, like all muffins, they are best eaten on the day that they're made.

Ingredients

80g (1/2 cup + 1 tablespoon) brown rice flour

30g (1/4 cup + 1 tablespoon) ground hazelnuts

30g (just under 1/2 cup) cocoa powder

1 teaspoon baking powder

1/4 teaspoon bicarbonate of soda

1/2 teaspoon salt

1/2 teaspoon espresso powder

1 large egg

75g (1/4 cup + 1 tablespoon) demerara sugar

1/2 teaspoon vanilla bean paste or vanilla extract

60ml (1/4 cup) extra virgin olive oil

60ml (1/4 cup) sour cream

50g (2 oz) dark chocolate, chopped

Crushed hazelnuts, to scatter on top

Directions

Preheat the oven to 170C/325F (fan) and line a muffin tin with paper cases.

In a large bowl, lightly whisk together the flour, ground hazelnuts, cocoa powder, baking powder, bicarbonate of soda, salt, and espresso powder. In another bowl, whisk together the egg, sugar, vanilla, olive oil and sour cream. Pour the wet ingredients over the dry ingredients and gently fold a couple of times. Add the chocolate chips and fold again until the streaks of flour just disappear.

Spoon the batter into the muffin cases, sprinkle with chopped hazelnuts and bake for 20 - 15 minutes until risen and firm to the touch. Allow to cool in the pan for 10 minutes or so before removing.

NOTES

Fairly heavily adapted from canelle et vanille's blueberry, lemon and olive oil muffins. For a dairy-free option, use coconut milk rather than sour cream and dairy-free chocolate chips.

Apple Pie Muffins

YIELD: 12 muffins
PREP TIME: 20 minutes; COOK TIME: 25 minutes

Ingredients

2 1/4 cups all-purpose flour

2 teaspoons pumpkin pie spice

1 teaspoon baking soda

1/2 teaspoon kosher salt

1 egg

1 cup buttermilk

1/2 cup butter, melted

1 teaspoon vanilla extract

1 1/2 cups packed brown sugar

2 cups peeled, chopped Granny Smith Apples

For the Topping

1/2 cup packed brown sugar

1/3 cup all-purpose flour

¼ cup rolled oats

1 teaspoon ground cinnamon

3 tablespoons butter, melted

Directions

1. Preheat the oven to 375 degrees F. Line 12 cup muffin cups with paper liners. Set aside.

2. In a large bowl, whisk together 2 1/4 cups flour, pumpkin pie spice, baking soda, and salt. In a small bowl, whisk together the egg, buttermilk, 1/2 cup melted butter, vanilla and 1 1/2 cups of brown sugar. Stir until sugar has dissolved.

3. Pour butter mixture into the flour mixture and stir until just combined. Gently fold in apples. Use a large scoop to fill each muffin well, filling the cups to the top.

4. In a small bowl, stir together 1/2 cup of brown sugar, 1/3 cup flour, rolled oats, and cinnamon. Drizzle in 3 tablespoons of melted butter, mixing until well blended. Sprinkle this over the tops of the muffins.

5. Bake in preheated oven for 25 minutes, or until the tops of the muffins spring back when lightly pressed.

6. Cool on wire rack. Store at room temperature.

Notes:

- If you choose to finely dice your apples, take not that they will disappear into the muffin. I left my pieces a little bigger to ensure nice bites of appley goodness.

- If you don't have pumpkin pie spice, you can make your own, or simply substitute 2 teaspoons of cinnamon.

-Recipe adapted from allrecipes.com

Triple Chocolate Muffins

YIELD: 24 muffins

Ingredients

2 cups plus 2 tablespoons all-purpose flour

3/4 cup unsweetened natural cocoa powder

1 tablespoon baking powder

1/2 teaspoon baking soda

1/4 teaspoon salt

2 large eggs

1 1/4 cups granulated sugar

1 cup buttermilk

1/2 cup (1 stick) unsalted butter, melted and cooled

1 teaspoon pure vanilla extract

4 ounces dark chocolate (70%) chunks

2 ounces mini semisweet chocolate chips

Directions

Preheat the oven to 400 (F) and prepare two muffin tins by lining each cavity with its own muffin liner.

In a medium bowl, whisk together 2 cups plus 2 tablespoons all-purpose flour, 3/4 cup unsweetened natural cocoa powder, 1 tablespoon baking powder, 1/2 teaspoon baking soda, and 1/4 teaspoon salt until combined. Set aside.

In a large bowl, whisk together 2 large eggs and 1 1/4 cups granulated sugar until a pale yellow. Add 1 cup buttermilk, 1/2 cup melted unsalted butter and 1 teaspoon pure vanilla extract and whisk until just combined.

Sprinkle the dry ingredients (from the 2nd step) evenly onto the surface of the wet ingredients (from the 3rd step). Use a rubber spatula to fold until combined, with one or two flour streaks left in the batter. Add 3 ounces dark chocolate chunks and 1 ounce mini chocolate chips (reserve the rest of the chocolate) and fold into the batter until just combined. DO NOT OVER MIX.

Divide the batter between 24 liners, using a 1 tablespoon cookie dough scoop to spoon about 2 tablespoons of batter per liner or at least until the liners are 2/3s of the way full. Sprinkle the tops of each muffin with the remaining chocolate pieces.

Bake in the preheated oven for 18 to 21 minutes or until the tops look set and a skewer inserted into the center of a muffin comes out almost clean. Allow the muffins to cool in the tin on a wire rack for 10 minutes, before turning out onto the wire rack to cool completely.

Banana Macadamia Nut Muffins

YIELD: 12 muffins

PREP TIME: 20 minutes; COOK TIME: 25 minutes

TOTAL TIME: 55 minutes

Fabulous banana muffins that taste like banana bread, loaded with macadamia nuts in the batter and on top of the muffins.

Ingredients

1½ cups unbleached all-purpose flour

1½ teaspoons baking soda

¼ teaspoon salt

⅛ teaspoon ground nutmeg

1¼ cups mashed ripe bananas (about 3 large)

½ cup granulated sugar

¼ cup dark brown sugar

½ cup unsalted butter, melted and cooled slightly

¼ cup milk (whole, 2% or 1%)

1 large egg

1 cup unsalted macadamia nuts, toasted and finely chopped

Directions

1. Preheat oven to 350 degrees F. Line a standard-size muffin pan with paper liners or spray with non-stick cooking spray; set aside.

2. Sift together the flour, baking soda, salt and nutmeg into a large bowl.

3. In a separate medium bowl, whisk together the mashed bananas, both sugars, butter, milk and egg. Pour over the dry ingredients and fold to combine. Add half of the chopped macadamia nuts to the batter and fold gently to combine.

4. Divide the batter evenly between the muffin cups. Sprinkle the tops with the remaining chopped macadamia nuts.

5. Bake until golden brown and a thing knife inserted into the center comes out clean, about 25 minutes. Let cool in the muffin pan for about 10 minutes, then remove to a wire rack to cool completely. Store muffins at room temperature for up to 3 days.

(Recipe from Epicurious)

S'mores Muffins

Ingredients

2 cups flour

1/3 cup light brown sugar

1/3 cup sugar

1/2 teaspoon salt

2 teaspoons baking powder

1/2 cup butter, melted

1/2 cup marshmallow fluff

2 eggs

2/3 cup soy milk (can substitute regular milk)

1 teaspoon vanilla

1/2 cup graham crackers, crushed (can have some pieces)

2/3 cup mini chocolate chips

Graham Cracker Streusel

1/4 cup flour

1/4 cup brown sugar

1/2 graham crackers, crushed

1/2 teaspoon cinnamon

2 tablespoons butter, melted

Directions

Preheat the oven to 400 degrees.

In a large-sized bowl whisk together the flour, brown sugar, sugar, salt, and baking powder.

In a medium-sized bowl whisk together the butter, marshmallow fluff, eggs, milk, and vanilla until they are well combined. (The marshmallow fluff may not completely combine and may be a little clumpy until it is mixed with the dry ingredients).

Slowly pour the dry ingredients into the liquid ingredients and stir until combined. Once combined, gently fold in the graham crackers and mini chocolate chips.

Line 12 muffin cups with liners. Evenly divide the batter into the muffin liners.

Graham Cracker Streusel

In a medium sized bowl combine the flour, brown sugar, graham crackers, and cinnamon.

Add the melted butter and mix until crumbly. It should look like wet sand.

Top each muffin with 1 tablespoon of topping.

Bake the muffins for 17-20 minutes or until a toothpick inserted in the center comes out clean.

Cool for 5 minutes then remove the muffins and continue to cool on a wire rack. Store in an airtight container. If desired, when serving heat up in the microwave for about 15 seconds to melt the chocolate.

Cheddar + Brown Sugar Cornbread Muffins

YIELD: 12 muffins

Ingredients

1 cup whole wheat pastry flour

1 cup finely ground cornmeal

1 tablespoon baking powder

½ teaspoon salt

3 tablespoons brown sugar

1/4 cup creamed corn

1/2 cup butter, melted

1/2 cup milk

1/3 cup heavy cream or half and half

1 egg

1/3 cup freshly & finely grated cheddar cheese

Directions

Preheat the oven to 425 degrees F.

Combine flour, cornmeal, sugar, salt and baking powder together and mix with a spoon. Add the egg, corn, heavy cream, melted butter and milk, stirring until smooth. Fold in cheddar cheese. Spray a muffin tin with non-stick spray (or use liners) and using a 1/4 cup measure, spoon batter into each muffin tin. Bake for 15-18 muffins, or until tops are golden and muffins are cooked through. Serve hot with cinnamon or honey butter.

[adapted from my fluffy delicious cornbread]

Jumbo Lemon Coffee Cake Muffins

YIELD: 6 jumbo or 12 regular muffins

Ingredients

2 cups All Purpose Flour

1 teaspoon Baking Powder

1 teaspoon Baking Soda

1 teaspoon Kosher Salt

1/2 cup Unsalted Butter, softened at room temperature {plus more for pans}

1 cup Sugar

1 tablespoon Lemon Zest {or about four lemons}

2 large Eggs

1 teaspoon Real Vanilla Extract

1 cup Buttermilk

{For the Streusel}

1 3/4 cup All-purpose flour

3/4 cup light brown sugar

1 teaspoon Kosher Salt

3/4 cup Unsalted butter, chilled

For the Glaze

1 cup Powdered Sugar

3 tablespoons Lemon Juice, freshly squeezed

Directions

Start by preheating oven to 350 degrees and buttering a large muffin tin. In a medium bowl prepare the streusel by mixing the flour, light brown sugar and salt. With a pastry cutter, cut in 3/4 cup of chilled butter and refrigerate until ready to use.

For the muffins; in a large bowl whisk together the flour, baking soda, baking powder and salt, set aside. Next beat the butter and sugar on medium low until light and creamy. Add the zest and with the mixer on low slowly blend one egg at a time, scraping down the sides and bottom of the bowl in between. Lastly add the vanilla. Once blended add a third of the buttermilk, then a third of the flour mixture alternating until all incorporated.

Divide the batter among the 6 muffin cups and then sprinkle with the streusel. Place the filled muffin tin in a preheated oven for 45-55 minutes, or until done. Check by inserting a tooth pick or cake tester, they are done when it comes out clean. Let cool completely.

Prepare the glaze by whisking the powdered sugar with fresh lemon juice. Let sit for a few minutes to thicken slightly then with a spoon drizzle over muffin tops. Serve!

Quinoa Muffins

YIELD: 8 muffins

Ingredients

¼ cup canola or other oil

½ cup sugar minus 2 tablespoons

½ teaspoon vanilla

1 egg

1/8 teaspoon salt

½ teaspoon baking powder

¼ teaspoon baking soda

¾ cup flour

¾ teaspoon cinnamon

¼ cup almond milk

½ cup cooked quinoa

Coarse sugar for sprinkling (optional)

Directions

Preheat the oven to 350°F. In a large bowl, combine the oil with the sugar, vanilla, and egg. Beat until the mixture is smooth and slightly thickened. Add the almond milk and mix again.

On a plate or in a small bowl, combine the flour, salt, baking powder, baking soda, cinnamon and salt. Sprinkle this over the wet ingredients, and fold together. Add the quinoa and stir to combine.

Divide the batter evenly among 8 muffin cups. (Fill the remaining cups with water to protect your pan.)

Bake for 20 minutes, until the muffins have risen and a toothpick inserted into the center of the muffin comes out clean. Serve warm or room temp.

Ginger Muffins with Dark Chocolate Glaze

YIELD: 12 muffins

PREP TIME: 20 minutes; COOK TIME: 20 minutes

Ingredients

1 1/2 cups all-purpose flour

2 teaspoons baking powder

1/2 teaspoon baking soda

1/2 teaspoon salt

1 cup granulated sugar

1 stick unsalted butter, melted, cooled

1/3 cup buttermilk + 2 tablespoons

2 large eggs

2 teaspoons pure vanilla extract

1 cup dark chocolate chips

1 tablespoon crystallized ginger, + more for garnish

Directions

Preheat oven to 350 degrees. In a medium bowl, mix all the dry ingredients. In another medium bowl, mix together sugar, butter, buttermilk, eggs, and vanilla exact. Add dry ingredients to wet ingredients a 1/3 at time until the flour has been incorporated. Stir in the chocolate chips and crystallized ginger.

Line a 12 cup muffin tin with cupcake liners. Take an ice cream scoop, and scoop out the batter and fill each liner. Bake for about 15 minutes or until you insert a toothpick and it comes out clean. Remove from oven and set aside to cool on a wire rack.

Once the chocolate glaze has slightly cool, take a knife and spread some of the glaze on top of the muffin. Garish with a sprinkle of crystallized ginger!

CHOCOLATE GLAZE

Ingredients

1/2 cup dark chocolate chips

2 tablespoons butter

2 tablespoons corn syrup

2 teaspoons hot water

Directions

In a medium saucepan, add chocolate, butter, and corn syrup. Melt over low heat, stirring so it doesn't burn. Add a teaspoon of water to thin it out. Set aside to cool slightly.

Adapted from food and wine magazine

Mocha Muffins

Author: The Crepes of Wrath

PREP TIME: 45 minutes; COOK TIME: 25 minutes

TOTAL TIME: 1 hour 10 minutes

Ingredients

2 cups + 2 tablespoons all-purpose flour

⅔ cup granulated sugar

⅓ cup unsweetened cocoa powder

2 tablespoons finely ground coffee beans

1 tablespoon baking powder

½ teaspoon baking soda

½ teaspoon kosher salt

6 tablespoons unsalted butter, cubed

5 ounces dark chocolate, roughly chopped (or chocolate chips)

1 and ¼ cups whole milk, room temperature

1 large egg, room temperature

2 teaspoons coffee extract

8 ounces dark chocolate, roughly chopped (or chocolate chips)

Raw sugar, for sprinkling (optional)

Directions

Preheat your oven to 375 degrees F and line your muffin pans. Place your butter and 5 ounces of chocolate in a medium sized pot, place over medium-low heat, and stir constantly for 5-8 minutes or so, until melted. If you have a double boiler, definitely use that, but I find that as long as you keep a watchful eye over your chocolate, you can just melt it straight in the pot. When it is smooth, set aside and allow to cool for at least 15 minutes.

In a separate bowl, whisk together your flour, sugar, cocoa powder, ground coffee beans, baking powder, baking soda, and salt, then set aside. In the bowl of your mixer, beat together the milk, egg, and coffee extract, then gradually add in the chocolate and butter mixture, stirring gently until combined (this is why your eggs and milk need to be at room temperature - if they are too cold, the chocolate will immediately harden and your batter will not be smooth).

Add in your flour mixture, a bit at a time, mixing until the batter is just moistened. Fold in your remaining chopped chocolate or chocolate chips, then divide the batter evenly among your muffin cups and sprinkle each one with a bit of raw sugar, if you like. Bake for 20-22 minutes, until a toothpick comes out clean and the tops are slightly crackled and set. Allow to cool completely in the tins before removing. These will keep well in an airtight container at room temperature for up to 3 days.

Salute to 35+ Moms & Work at Home Moms Week Tips Handout

Designed by DocUmeantDesigns.com

MAY 14-20
Salute to 35+ Moms & Work at Home Moms Week Tips

11 Tips for Work At Home Moms

1. Get your baby on a schedule
2. Create rituals
3. Keep a running To Do list with daily action items
4. Set timers
5. Make use of drive time
6. Schedule walking meetings
7. Wake up early
8. Only respond to emails that truly need a response
9. Prep on Sundays
10. Hire help
11. Remain flexible

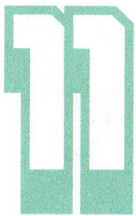

11 Way To Start Earning a Side Income from Home

1. Start a Free Amazon Associates Account
2. Freelance Writing for Blogs or articles
3. Put Money in a Retirement Fund
4. Sell Crafts on Etsy, eBay, or Amazon Associates
5. Start a Blog
6. Be a Virtual Assistant
7. Photography
8. Arbitrage for Amazon FBA
9. Write an eBook
10. Flip items on Craigslist
11. Contests
Bonus: Sign up for Survey Sites

[Your Business Info Here • Website • eMail]

National Nightshift/Thirdshift Workers Day Card

Designed by DocUmeantDesigns.com

These can be printed several per page. You can create them in 3 x 5-inch cards or business card size. If you want the printable file, email me at support@holidaymarketinguide.com.

Business Card

3 x 5-inch card

National Odometer Day Card

Designed by DocUmeantDesigns.com

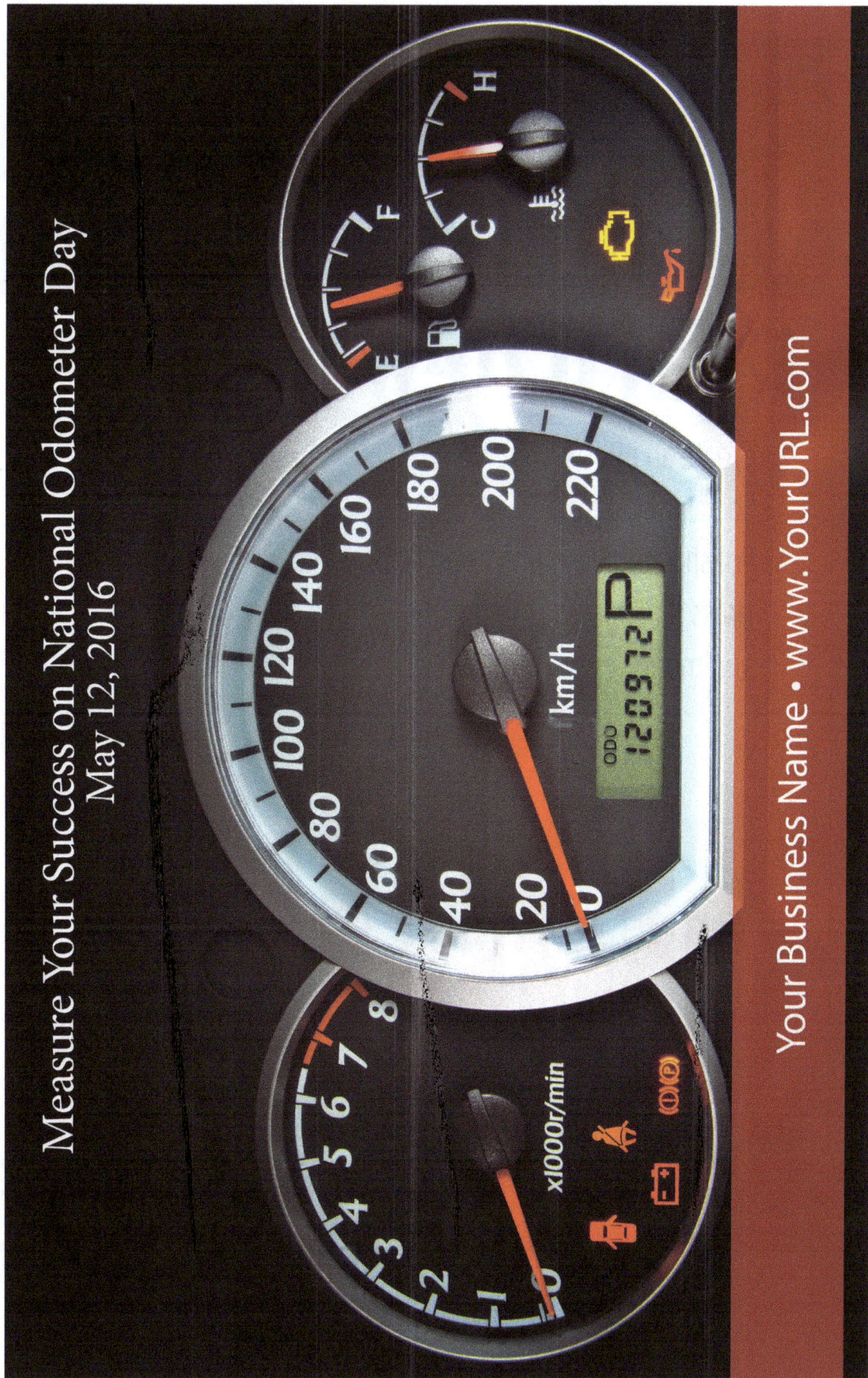

Measure Your Success on National Odometer Day
May 12, 2016

Your Business Name • www.YourURL.com

Skyscraper Event Flier

Designed by DocUmeantDesigns.com

Join us for
Skyscraper Month
Challenge
June 1-30, 2016

Reach new heights

- Create an eBook
- Social media tips
- Polish your communication skills
- Dress for Success Training
- and more!

For more information and to register visit:

How to Hug Your Cat Poster

Note: I would give credit if I could read who created this. ;-)

Ways to Hug a Cat

Teddy Hug

Belly Hug

Strangle Hug

Burp Hug

Condolence Hug

Ledge Hug

Face Hug

Heat Pad Hug

Work @ Home Father's Day Graphic

Designed by DocUmeantDesigns.com

Work @ Home Father's Day Essay Contest Flier

Designed by DocUmeantDesigns.com

Work @ Home Fathers Day
June 16

Why i Work @ Home:
A Dad's View Essay Contest

Entrants must be fathers with at least one in-home, minor child, and must work or telework from a home office at least one day each week. Prizes include:

To Enter:
Submit your 250-word essay on how working from home has improved the balance between your family and professional life.

Deadline: June 1 Midnight EST

Submit your essay to:
Your email/fax/or snail mail information

Sponsors:

Your Business info here

Caribbean Day Fill in the Blank

Song Titles

Give extra points for naming the artist. I have ordered these by artists, so be sure to mix them up to add to the fun.

1. ___ ___ ___ ___   ___ ___ ___ ___ ___ ___
2. ___ ___ ___ ___ ___ ___ ___ ___ ___ ___ ___ ___ ___
3. ___ ___ ___ ___ ___
4. ___ ___ ___   ___ ___ ___   ___ ___ ___ ___
5. ___ ___ ___ ' ___   ___ ___ ___ ___ ___   ___ ___ ___   ___ ___ ___ ___ ___
6. ___ ___ ___ ___ ___ ___ ___ ___
7. ___ ___ ___ ___ ___ ___
8. ___ ___ ___ ___
9. ___ ___ ___ ___ ___ ___ ___ ___   ___ ___ ___   ___ ___
   ___ ___ ___ ___ ___ ___ ___
10. ___ ___ ___ ___ ___ ___ ___ ___   ___ ___ ___ ___   ___
11. ___ ___   ___ ___ ___ ___ ___   ___ ___ ___ ___ ___
12. ___ ___ ___ ___ ___ ___
13. ___ ___ ___ ___ ___   ___ ___ ___ ___ ___ ___   ___ ___ ___ ___ ___
14. ___ ___ ___ ___   ___ ___ ___   ___ ___
15. ___ ___ ___   ___ ___ ___ ___
16. ___ ___ ___ - ___
17. ___ ___ ___ ___ ___ ___ ___   ___ ___ ___ ___ ___ ___ ___ ___
18. ___ ___ ___ ___ ___ ___ ___
19. ___ ___ ___ ___   ___ ___ ___   ___ ___ ___   ___ ___ ___ ___
20. ___ ___ ___ ___ ___ ___ ___   ___ ___ ___ ___ ___

Answers

1. Jimmy Buffett: "Boat Drinks"
2. Jimmy Buffett: "Margaritaville"
3. The Beach Boys: "Kokomo"
4. UB40: "Red Red Wine"
5. Bobby McFerrin: "Don't Worry, Be Happy"
6. Harry Nilsson: "Coconut"
7. Pharrell Williams: "Happy"
8. Zac Brown Band: "Toes"
9. Phil Collins: "Another Day In Paradise"
10. Sade: "The Sweetest Taboo"
11. Bob Marley: "Is this Love"
12. Bob Marley: "Jammin"
13. Bob Marley: "Three Little Birds"
14. Bob Marley: "Stir It Up"
15. Bob Marley: "One Love"
16. Harry Belafonte: "Day-O"
17. Harry Belafonte: "Jamaica Farewell"
18. Harry Belafonte: "Matilda"
19. Harry Belafonte: "Jump In The Line"
20. Calypso Rose: "Calypso Queen"

Caribbean Day Card

Designed by DocUmeantDesigns.com

Greeting Card Size Chart

To design your custom cards us the chart below. Be sure to extend your image 1/8" beyond the size if you wish your image to cover the entirety of your card. For the front only image you will not need the extra bleed on the inside edge.

If you need additional help in creating your card template to use or want help with your design a quick email is all you need to worry about. Send it to support@holidaymarketingguide.com and I'll get back to you promptly.

Card Base	Unfold	Folded	Envelope Size
A2 Notecards	8.5" x 5.5"	4.25" x 5.5"	4.375" x 5.625"
A6 Notecards	9.25" x 6.25"	4.625" x 6.25"	4.75" x 6.5"
A7 Greeting Card	10" x 7"	5" x 7"	5.25" x 7.25"
A9 Greeting Card	8.5" x 11"	8.5" x 5.5"	8.625" x 5.625"
Large Square	5.25" x 10.5"	5.25" x 5.25"	5.5" x 5.5"
Medium Square	9.5" x 4.75"	4.75" x 4.75"	5" x 5"
Small Square	3.25" x 6.5"	3.25 x 3.25"	3.5" x 3.5"
Tall	8.5" x 8.5"	8.5" x 4.25"	8.75" x4.375"
Skinny	8.5" x 7"	8.5" x 3.5"	8.75" x 3.75"
Gate Fold	8.5" x 10"	8.5" x 5" (flaps 2.5")	7.75" x 5.25"
Two-Fold Sm Square	3.75" x 11.25"	3.75" x 3.75	4" x 4"

Riot Act Day Button

Designed by DocUmeantDesigns.com

RIOT ACT DAY

I'M MAD AS HELL!
AND I'M NOT GUNNA TAKE IT
ANYMORE!

JULY 20

Baker's Dozen Rain Day Quotes

Courtesy of BrainyQuotes.com

1. Clouds come floating into my life, no longer to carry rain or usher storm, but to add color to my sunset sky. Rabindranath Tagore

2. Life is full of beauty. Notice it. Notice the bumble bee, the small child, and the smiling faces. Smell the rain, and feel the wind. Live your life to the fullest potential, and fight for your dreams. Ashley Smith

3. The best thing one can do when it's raining is to let it rain. Henry Wadsworth Longfellow

4. Sunshine is delicious, rain is refreshing, wind braces us up, snow is exhilarating; there is really no such thing as bad weather, only different kinds of good weather. John Ruskin

5. No person has the right to rain on your dreams. Marian Wright Edelman

6. The drops of rain make a hole in the stone, not by violence, but by oft falling. Lucretius

7. A crown is merely a hat that lets the rain in. Frederick the Great

8. The rain begins with a single drop. Manal al-Sharif

9. Sometimes we should express our gratitude for the small and simple things like the scent of the rain, the taste of your favorite food, or the sound of a loved one's voice. Joseph B. Wirthlin

10. Criticism, like rain, should be gentle enough to nourish a man's growth without destroying his roots. Frank A. Clark

11. Without rain, there is no life. Jerry Yang

12. Thy fate is the common fate of all; Into each life some rain must fall. Henry Wadsworth Longfellow

13. Life is not about waiting for the storm to pass, it's about learning to dance in the rain. Vivian Greene

Rain Day Poster

Designed by DocUmeantDesigns.com

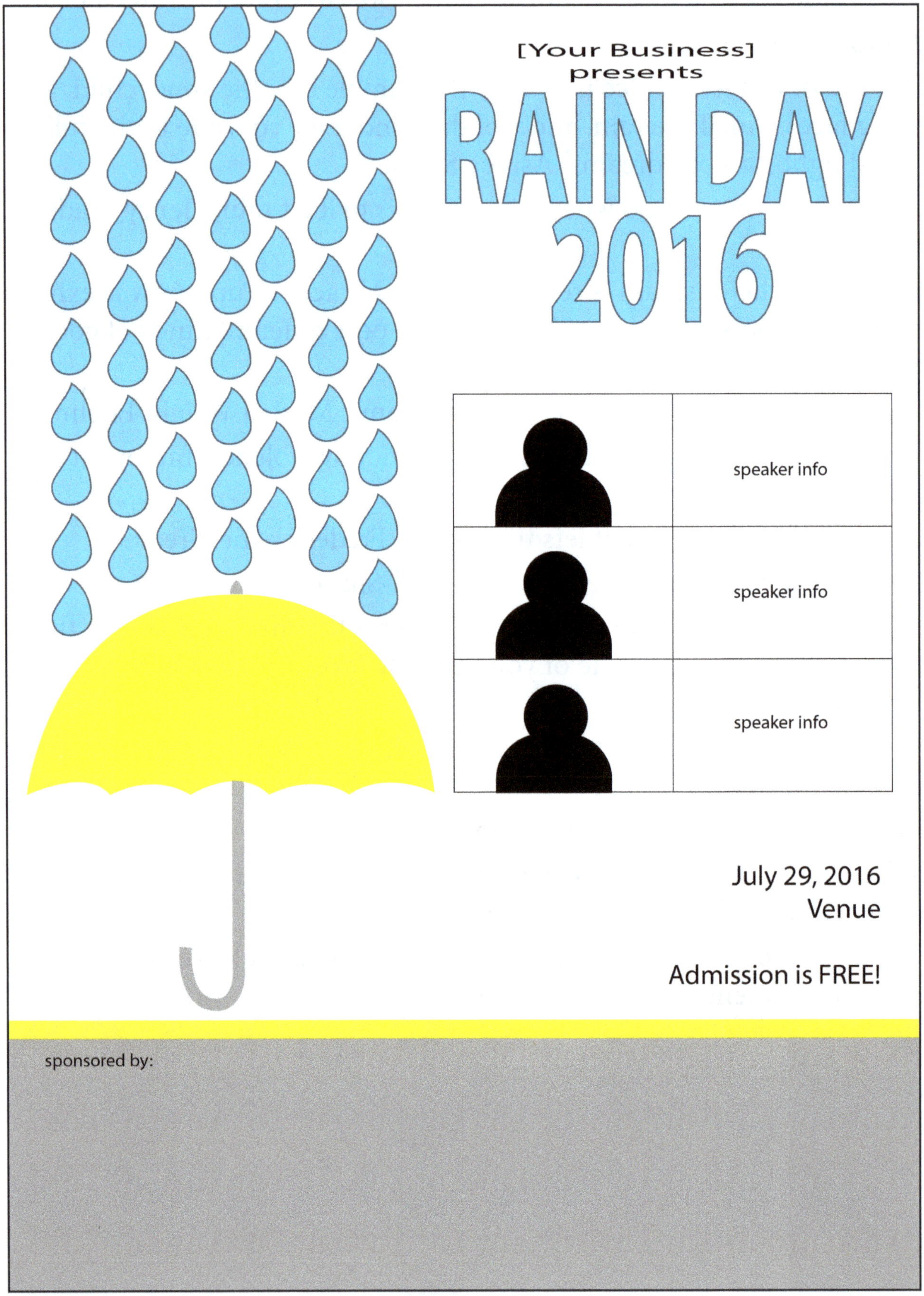

World Wide Web Day Card

Designed by DocUmeantDesigns.com

HAPPY WORLD WIDE WEB DAY

The World Wide Web was conceived by Tim Berners-Lee in 1989 at the CERN centre in Geneva, Switzerland, as a way for him to communicate with co-workers via hyperlinks.

August 1

[your company]

Left Hander's Day Activities

Courtesy of http://www.lefthandersday.com/

Declare an area (or all!) of your home or workplace a designated "Lefty Zone" where everyone must do all tasks left-handed.

Get your right handed friends, family and colleagues to do all daily tasks using their normal equipment, but with their left hand e.g.:

1. Stir food in pans
2. Fill & pour kettle
3. Pour from milk/measuring jugs
4. Open tins
5. Peel vegetables/fruit
6. Open wine bottles
7. Use microwave/hob controls (often positioned on right of the equipment)
8. Wash up (draining board is often wrong side if you are holding the brush in other hand, so you have to pass wet dishes across your body to drain.
9. Cutting bread (wonky slices using right handed knife in left hand)
10. Eating & drinking – reverse cutlery and have drink in left hand
11. Cutting – using right-handed scissors in left hand is an excellent example of totally right-biased design that doesn't work well.
12. Ironing with board & iron reversed – adults & older children only!
13. Drawing a measured line with a ruler
14. Having the computer mouse on the left of the keyboard and try drawing a shape on screen, or clicking and dragging – we usually have to do this with our right hand as the mouse is shared, and always set up for right-handed users
15. Use the computer keypad to enter lots of numbers – using wrong hand
16. Draw or write in ring binder / spiral bound notepad with left hand – binding hurts wrist
17. Using fountain/ink pen or just felts and color in with left hand – smudged work and ink on side of hand as it follows the work
18. If you have left handed guitar, give lessons to the right-handers.
19. Practice recorder or other instruments with hands reversed (top and bottom)

Left Hander's Zone Poster

Courtesy of http://www.lefthandersday.com/

WARNING:
You are now entering
a left-handed zone!

Use of right-hand for
everyday tasks is
strictly prohibited

August 13th   www.lefthandersday.com   #lefthandersday

Left Hander's Day Right Mind Poster

Courtesy of http://www.lefthandersday.com/left-handers-day/celebrate#.WCSP7C0rJR0

If the right side of the brain controls the left side of the body,

Mathematics

Language

Lists

Logic

Writing

Scientific Skills

Emotional Expression

Spatial Awareness

Creativity

Music

Imagination

Whole Picture

then only left-handers are in their right minds!

August 13th   www.lefthandersday.com   #lefthandersday

Race Your Mouse Around the Icons Day Graphic

Designed by DocUmeantDesigns.com

The 4 Principles of Hand Awareness

Courtesy of http://www.henrythehand.com/

This can easily be made into a card or flyer and branded with your company's logo. If you need help or don't know where to start email me at support@holidaymarketingguide.com.

1. Wash your hands when they are dirty and BEFORE eating
2. DO NOT cough into your hands
3. DO NOT sneeze into your hands
4. Above all, DO NOT put your fingers into your eyes, nose or mouth

The 4 Principles of Hand Awareness have been endorsed by the AMA and AAFP

The CDC and Prevention say hand washing is the single most effective way to prevent the transmission of disease.

The 4 Principles of Hand Awareness

Bison-Ten-Yell Card

Designed by DocUmeantDesigns.com

Wonderful Weirdos Day Photo Poster

Designed by DocUmeantDesigns.com

National Fossil Day Poster

Designed by DocUmeantDesigns.com

National
Fossil Day
of Discovery

Brush off the sediment covering your dreams to unearth your path to success in business.

You will learn:
• point one
• point two
• point three

Join us Oct 2, 2017
10:00 a.m to 3:00 p.m.
at: Location

[Your business info]

Feline Quotes

Courtesy of International Business Times article by Suman Varandani

"What greater gift than the love of a cat?" — Charles Dickens

"Time spent with a cat is never wasted." — Colette

"A cat has absolute emotional honesty: human beings, for one reason or another, may hide their feelings, but a cat does not." — Ernest Hemingway

"Cats know how to obtain food without labor, shelter without confinement, and love without penalties." — Walter Lionel George

"How we behave toward cats here below determines our status in heaven." — Robert A. Heinlein

"A cat can be trusted to purr when she is pleased, which is more than can be said for human beings." — William Ralph Inge

"Cats do not have to be shown how to have a good time, for they are unfailing ingenious in that respect." — James Mason

"I wish I could write as mysterious as a cat." — Edgar Allan Poe

"I have studied many philosophers and many cats. The wisdom of cats is infinitely superior." —Hippolyte Taine

"I love cats because I enjoy my home; and little by little, they become its visible soul." — Jean Cocteau

65 Catchy Animal Abuse and Cruelty Slogans

Courtesy of http://brandongaille.com/65-catchy-animal-abuse-and-cruelty-slogans/

For use on cards and posters.

1. A hamburger stops a beating heart.
2. Adopt, Rescue, Love forever.
3. Animal activists unite as one. We won't stop fighting until the war is won.
4. Animals are my friends and I don't wear my friends.
5. Animals are your neighbors on this earth- respect them!
6. Animals give me more pleasure through the viewfinder of a camera than they ever did in the crosshairs of a gunsight.
7. Animals, abuse them and you will lose them.
8. Are clothes to kill for?
9. Ask the experimenters why they experiment on animals, and the answer is: "Because the animals are like us." Ask the experimenters why it is morally okay to experiment on animals, and the answer is: "Because the animals are not like us."
10. Avoid a CATastrophe, spray or neuter.
11. Avoid getting caught in the fashion TRAP, Don't wear fur.
12. Be an everyday hero, stop animal abuse.
13. Be the voice they wish they had, make the choice they wish they could.
14. Being cruel isn't cool.
15. Cruelty is one fashion statement we can do without.
16. Do not buy animals from pet shops this increases puppy mills.
17. Do not neglect, protect! Slowly see the affect, as the animals reconnect!
18. Don't act blindly, treat us kindly.
19. don't be a loser, stop the abuser.
20. Don't breed or buy, while shelter animals die.
21. don't treat animals the way you don't want to be treated.
22. DONT CHOOSE TO ABUSE!
23. Eat beans not beings.
24. Evolve: End Violence Against Animals.
25. Fake for the animals sake.
26. Feed it, don't eat it.
27. For as long as men massacre animals, they will kill each other.
28. Friends don't chain friends.
29. Fur belongs to the animal that was wearing it first.
30. Fur is not fair.
31. Give a hoot, give fur the boot.
32. Give Peas a chance!
33. Give us truth and stop the abuse!
34. God loved the birds and created trees, humans loved the birds and created cages.
35. He who sows the seed of murder and pain cannot reap joy and love.

36. Humans aren't the only species on Earth, We just act like it!
37. Hunting is not a sport. In a sport, both sides should know they're in the game.
38. I rather go naked than wear fur.
39. If you are what you eat, does that make you Dead Meat!
40. If you had to kill the cow yourself, you'd eat tofu.
41. Killing for recreation is obscene.
42. Know Compassion, Know Peace.
43. Love me, don't eat me.
44. Never wear anything that panics the cat.
45. No compassion, No peace.
46. One can measure the greatness and moral progress of a nation by looking at how it treats its animals.
47. Our lives begin to end the day we become silent about things that matter.
48. People who abuse animals barely stop there.
49. Pets for Peace, not Beats.
50. Punish the deed, not the breed.
51. Real people wear fake fur.
52. Rescued is my favorite breed.
53. Save a Life, eat Tofu.
54. Take out the blindness, show a little kindness, evolve up the ladder, get conscious- animals matter.
55. The fascination of shooting as a sport depends on whether you are at the right or wrong end of a gun.
56. The question is not, "Can they reason?" nor, "Can they talk?" but rather, "Can they suffer?"
57. The time will come when men such as I will look upon the murder of animals as they now look on the murder of men.
58. There is no excuse for animal abuse.
59. Vegetarian because meat is murder.
60. We can judge the heart of a man by how he treats animals.
61. We will never find peace among people whose heart finds satisfaction in killing living things.
62. When a man destroys one of the works of man we call him a vandal. When he destroys one of the works of god we call him a sportsman.
63. Why should man expect his prayer for mercy to be heard by What is above him when he shows no mercy to what is under him?
64. Would you want to spend your entire life on a chain? neither do they.
65. You are not an environmentalist if you eat factory farmed animals.

Mischief Night Pins

Designed by DocUmeantDesigns.com

Grand Mischief Maker

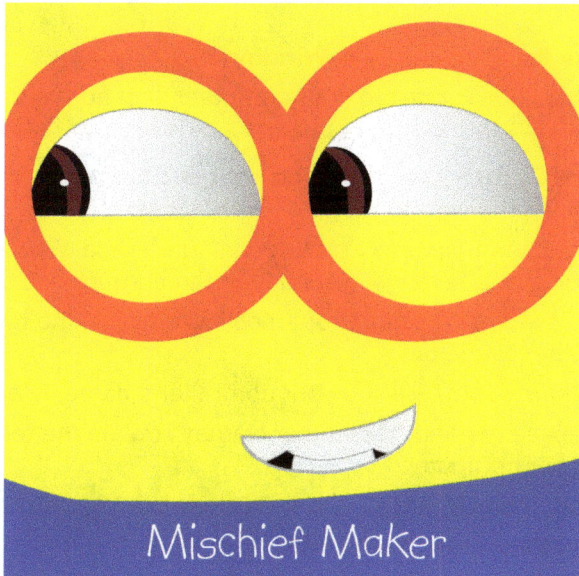

Mischief Maker

Name Your PC Day Card

Designed by DocUmeantDesigns.com

Happy Name Your PC Day!

HELLO
MY NAME IS
Old Faithful

How to change the name of your Windows PC

In Windows 10, 8.x, or 7, log into your computer with administrative rights.

Step 1: Navigate to the Control Panel.

Step 2: Click the System icon. (If you do not see the System icon, in the upper right corner, switch the view to Large or Small icons).

Step 3: In the "System" window that appears, under the "Computer name, domain and workgroup settings" section, on the right, click Change settings.

Step 4: You will see the "System Properties" window. At the top of the window, click the Computer Name tab.

Step 5: Click Change. You will see your computer's name listed.

Step 6: In the space marked "Computer Name:", delete the text and enter a new name for your computer.

Step 7: Click OK, then OK again, and then close the "System" window.

How to change the name of your Mac

Step 1: In the Menu bar, go to > System Preferences …

Step 2: Click on Sharing.

Step 3: In the Computer Name box, type in the name you want to use for your computer.

Step 4: Close the window, and you're done.

[Your Company • Your Company Website • Your Company contact info]

eCard Greeting

Designed by DocUmeantDesigns.com

eCard Greetings Day
[your business website]

November 29

Bingo Card

Designed by DocUmeantDesigns.com

YOUR LOGO

[YOUR BUSINESS INFO SPONSORS ETC HERE]

BINGO

FREE SPACE

Happy Birthday to Bingo Month

International Mountain Day Flier

Designed by DocUmeantDesigns.com

Tick Tock Day Card

Designed by DocUmeantDesigns.com

Appendix B: LINKS

Link Checker

For Chrome: https://chrome.google.com/webstore/detail/check-my-links/ojkcdipcgfaekbeaelaapakgnjflf-glf?hl=en-GB (I know this is out of alpha order, but a good link deserves top billing, don't you think? ;)

Article Marketing Sites

http://goarticles.com/

http://internationalpractice.com/business/

http://thephantomwriters.com/index.php

http://www.articledashboard.com/

http://www.articlegarden.com/

http://www.articlesbase.com/

http://www.articleson.com/

http://www.sitepronews.com/

http://www.selfgrowth.com

http://marniemarcus.com/unplugged/facebook-ad-management/

http://www.isnare.com

http://www.ladypens.com/

http://www.promotionworld.com

http://wahm–articles.com

http://www.writeandpublishyourbook.com/magazine/

https://contributor.yahoo.com/signup.shtml

http://www.ezinearticles.com

Auto Responder Services

AWeber: www.aweber.com/

Constant Contact: www.constantcontact.com/

Robly: https://app.robly.com/invite?rc=f56a53fb2ad6910f3e83ebda

Your Mailing List Provider: www.yourmailinglistprovider.com/

Books & Movies

The Home Owner's Manual: Operating Instructions, Troubleshooting Tips, and Advice on System
 Maintenance by Dan Ramsey: https://www.amazon.com/dp/1594741034/

Madly In Love With Me by Christine Arylo: http://madlyinlovewithme.com/books/#booktrailer

Complete Library of Entrepreneurial Wisdom: http://www.CLEWbook.com

Operation North Pole Days: http://youtu.be/27I63MY3H_A

Presentational Skills for the Next Generation: http://www.amazon.com/dp/B005EA01QO

The Better Hour: The Legacy of William Wilberforce: http://www.thebetterhour.org/tbh/index.htm

Greeting Card Companies

123Greetings: http://www.123greetings.com

American Greetings: http://www.americangreetings.com/

Blue Mountain: www.bluemountain.com/

Cyberkisses: http://www.cyberkisses.com/

Day Springs: www.dayspring.com/ecards/

Evite: www.evite.com

Hallmark: http://www.hallmark.com/

Jacquie Lawson: www.jacquielawson.com/

Just Wink:_https://www.justwink.com/

Operation Write Home: http://operationwritehome.org/

Punchbowl Greetings: http://www.punchbowl.com/invitations/preview/5400a4b424e4b36a3e000029/5
 400a56bbf947f655a000111

Send Out Cards: www.sendoutcards.com/

Podcast Directories

Corante-Podcasting: http://podcasting.corante.com/—Weblog with news and events related to podcasting.

Hipcast: http://www.hipcaStcom/—Audio and video podcasting service. Includes news and on-line tour.

iTunes: http://blog.lextext.com/blog/_archives/2005/1/4/225172.html—The iTunes Store puts thousands
 of free podcasts at your fingertips.

Lextext.com: How to Podcast RIAA Music Under License—http://blog.lextext.com/blog/_
 archives/2005/1/4/225172.html—Discussion of legal ways to podcast music. [Podcast is 5.3
 MB in size]

The Liberated Syndication Network: http://www.libsyn.com/—Full featured service tailored specifically for
 media Self-publishing and podcasting. Price is based on usage, changing monthly if needed.

NPR: http://www.npr.org/rss/podcast/podcast_directory.php—Over 50 public radio stations and producers
 are working with NPR to bring you podcasting.

The Podcast Directory: http://www.podcastdirectory.com/—Up to date and relevant podcast directory.

Podcasting News: http://www.podcastingnews.com/—Information relating to podcasting, a podcast
 directory, and a user forum.

SkypeCasters: http://www.henshall.com/blog/archives/001056.html—Introducing instructions for SkypeCasting, the solution for podcasters to create audio recordings from interviews and conference calls using Skype.

Skype Forums: http://forum.skype.com/viewtopic.php?t=12788—Recording a Skype Conversation–Discussion thread covering software, techniques, and legal tidbits.

Wikipedia: Podcast –http://en.wikipedia.org/wiki/Podcast—Encyclopedia entry covering basics of the topic.

Promotional Product Supply Companies

4imprint: https://www.4imprint.com/ —offers free samples

Build A Sign: http://www.buildasign.com/

CafePress: www.cafepress.com/

Crown Awards: https://www.crownawards.com/

iPrint: http://www.iprint.com

Judie Glenn Inc: www.judieglenninc.com—ask for Tracey Arehart

Northwest Territorial Mint: http://custom.nwtmint.com/

Overnight Prints: http://www.overnightprints.com/

PC/Nametag®: http://www.pcnametag.com/

Promotional Products: www.promotionalproducts.org/—Get free quotes from multiple vendors

Staples: www.StaplesPromotionalProducts.com

VistaPrint: www.Vistaprint.com

World Class Medals : http://www.worldclassmedals.com/

Zazzle: http://www.zazzle.com/custom/buttons

Quote Sources

Bartleby: http://www.bartleby.com/

Brainy Quote: http://www.brainyquote.com/quotes/keywords/resources.html

Leadership Now: http://www.leadershipnow.com/quotes.html

Quote Garden: http://www.quotegarden.com/index.html

Quoteland: http://www.quoteland.com/

The Quotations Page: http://www.quotationspage.com/

Think Exit: http://thinkexist.com/quotes/american_proverb/

Woopidoo!: http://www.woopidoo.com/

Singing Telegram Services

Aarons Singing Telegrams: http://www.SingingTelegramsLosAngeles.com

American Singing Telegrams: http://www.americansingingtelegrams.com/

Gig Masters Singing Telegrams: http://www.gigmasters.com/SingingTelegram/Singing-Telegram.htm

Happy Entertainment Party Productions: http://www.happyentertainment.com/

The International Singing Telegram Company: http://balloonstunesworldwide.com/

Orange Peel Moses: http://www.customsingingtelegrams.com/

PreppyGrams Singing Telegrams: http://www.preppygrams.com/specialdelivery.html

Sunshine Singing Telegram Service: http://www.sunshinesingingtelegrams.com

The International Singing Telegram Company Inc.: https://www.facebook.com/pages/
The-International-Singing-Telegram-Company-Inc/173670102142

Wacky Jack's Singing Telegrams & Balloons: http://www.wackyjacktelegrams.com/

Stock Photos

Tiny Eye: http://www.tineye.com — Reverse image search

Beinecke: http://beinecke.library.yale.edu/digitallibrary

Maps Download MrSid: http://memory.loc.gov/ammem/help/download_sid.html

Big Stock Photo: http://www.bigstockphoto.com

Bing: http://www.bing.com

Can Stock Photo: http://www.canstockphoto.com

CreStock: http://www.crestock.com

DepositPhotos: http://depositphotos.com

Digital Scriptorium: http://bancroft.berkeley.edu/digitalscriptorium — public domain

Dreamstime: https://www.dreamstime.com

EJ Photo: http://www.ejphoto.com — Nature photography

Flickr: https://www.flickr.com — Advanced Search - only search on commercial content (etc)

Fotolia: http://www.foltolia.com

Foto Search: http://www.fotosearch.com

Free Digital Photos: http://www.freedigitalphotos.net

Free Photo: http://www.freefoto.com/index.jsp

Getty: http://www.gettyimages.com/

Google: http://www.images.google.com — Use Advanced Search for Usage Rights, labeled with commercial w/ modifications

Icon Finder: http://www.iconfinder.com/illustrations

iStockPhoto: http://www.iStockPhoto.com

Jupiter: http://www.jupiterimages.com

Library of Congress: http://www.loc.gov/index.html — American Memory and Prints & Photographs sections

Morguefile: http://morguefile.com

MyAlamy: http://www.alamy.com

PhotoSpin: https://www.photospin.com/Default.asp?

Pixabay: http://pixabay.com/

Pixadus: http://pixdaus.com

RGB Stock: www.rgbstock.com — more than 95,000 high quality free stock photos, graphics for illustrations, wallpapers, and backgrounds

Scriptorium: http://www.scriptorium.columbia.edu/public domain

Shutterstock: http://www.shutterstock.com

Stockxchg (FreeImages): http://www.sxc.hu/

ThinkStock Photos: http://www.thinkstockphotos.com/

Top Left Pixel: http://wvs.topleftpixel.com

Visipix: http://www.visipix.com — lots of Japanese art

Visual Photos: http://www.visualphotos.com

Watercolor Textures: https://lostandtaken.com/downloads/category/paint/watercolor-texture/

WebStockPro: http://www.webstockpro.com/

Wikimedia Commons: http://commons.wikimedia.org/wiki/Main_Page — Check images via languages

Wikipedia Public Domain List: http://en.wikipedia.org/wiki/Wikipedia:Public_domain_image_resources/ public domain

You Work for Them: http://www.youworkforthem.com

Teleconference Companies

What is: www.business.com/directory/telecommunications/business_solutions/conferencing/ Buyer's Guide: www.buyerzone.com/telecom_services/telecon_services/buyers_guide5.html Free Conference: www.freeconference.com/

Teleconference Live: http://teleconference.liveoffice.com

Teleconferencing Services: www.teleconferencingservices.net/

Wholesale Conference Call: www.wholesaleconferencecall.com/

Yugma Desktop Sharing Software: http://vur.me/gmarks/Yugma/

Virtual Assistant Companies

A Clayton's Secretary (Kathie M Thomas): http://vadirectory.net/

Collins Administrative Services (Tracy Collins): http://www.collins–admin.com

MJ Stern, VA: http://www.mjstern–va.com/—Specializes in Internet marketing

Streamline Your Marketing (Crystal Pina): http://www.streamlineyourmarketing.com

Virtual Freedom 4 You (Corrie Petersen): http://virtualfreedom4you.com/

Webinar Services

Adobe Acrobat Connect Pro: http://tryit.adobe.com/us/connectpro/universalvoice/?sdid=DNOSU

BrainShark: http://brainshark.com/

Cisco WebEx: http://webex.com/

ClickWebinar: http://www.clickwebinar.com/

DimDim: http://www.dimdim.com/

Elluminate: http://www.elluminate.com/Products/?id=3

Freebinar: http://www.freebinar.com/

Free Conference Calling: http://www.freeconferencecalling.com/

Fuze: http://www.fuzemeeting.com/

GatherPlace: http://www.gatherplace.net/start/

Google+ Hangouts: https://plus.google.com/hangouts

GoToMeeting: https://www.gotomeeting.com/

GoToWebinar: http://www.gotomeeting.com/fec/webinar

IBM Lotus Unyte: https://www.unyte.net/

iLinc: http://www.ilinc.com/

Infinite Conference: http://www.infiniteconference.com/

InstantPresenter: http://www.instantpresenter.com/

Intercall: http://www.intercall.com/smb/

Mega Meeting: http://www.megameeting.com/professional.html

Microsoft Office Live Meeting: http://www.microsoft.com/on-line/officE-livE-meeting/buy.mspx

Nefsis: http://www.nefsis.com/

Peter Pan Birthday Club: http://www.sjbhealth.org/body_foundation.cfm?id=1875

ReadyTalk: http://www.readytalk.com/

Saba Centra: http://saba.com/

StageToWeb: http://www.stagetoweb.com/livE-event–webcasting.html

Tokbox: http://tokbox.com/

Video Seminar Live: http://www.videoseminarlive.com/

Wix: http://www.wix.com/

Yugma: https://www.yugma.com/

Zoho: http://www.zoho.com/meeting/

Appendix C: RESOURCES

ADSHA: http://www.asha.org/bhsm/Ideas-to-Recognize-BHSM/

ARS: http://www.americanrecorder.org/play_the_recorder_month.php

As A Man Thinketh: http://asamanthinketh.net/

Cleaning Institue: Hand washing promo kit: http://www.cleaninginstitute.org/cleanhandspublications/

Clothes for Kids: http://www.clothestokids.org/

Constantly Speaking: http://www.consonantlyspeaking.com/2012/05/free-printables-for-better-hearing-and.html

Funnier than Grading: http://funnierthangrading.blogspot.com/)

HashifyMe: http://hashtagify.me/

Highway History: https://www.fhwa.dot.gov/infrastructure/numbers.cfm

Highway Signs: https://en.wikipedia.org/wiki/Numbered_highways_in_the_United_States

International Association of Skateboard Companies (IASC): http://theiasc.org/go-skateboarding-day/

Licorice International: http://www.licoriceinternational.com/

Love is Respect: http://www.loveisrespect.org/

Learn to Play the Recorder: http://www.arta-recorder.org/

Meanin of Names: http://www.meaning-of-names.com/

Movember: https://us.movember.com/

Muffin Recipes: https://www.bustle.com/articles/16156-celebrate-national-muffin-day-with-these-11-awesome-muffin-recipes

National Park Services, National Fossil Day: http://nature.nps.gov/geology/nationalfossilday/index.cfm

Note card Stock: https://www.thepapermillstore.com/notecards

Our Spaces: http://www.ourspaces.org.uk/activities.html

Philosophy Foundation: https://www.philosophy-foundation.org/

Stack a Badge Ribbons: http://www.pcnametag.com/category/7/badge-ribbons

TDV Resources: http://charmeck.org/mecklenburg/county/CommunitySupportServices/WomensCommission/Services/ChildrenServices/Pages/TDVResources.aspx

Unesco: http://en.unesco.org/events/world-philosophy-day-2015-roundtable-plurality-languages-and-places-philosophy

Welcome Card: http://www.welcomecard.biz/

About the Author

Having been a business owner for most of her adult life, operating a multi–million dollar surgical clinic and a local barbecue take-out to list just a couple, have given Ginger Marks the insight needed to assist business owners from all walks of life.

Ginger is the owner of the Calomar, LLC which holds her DocUmeant family of companies. The various entities all work towards a common goal that just happens to be their tagline; "We Make YOU Look GOOD!" Her services include both publishing and digital design assistance. She is proud of the fact that she is able to give high quality, efficient service at a remarkably reasonable rate. It is for this reason she chose to list her publishing company in New York City while residing in Florida.

When Ginger decided to embark on a writing career it was of no surprise to her mother, who herself is a published author. Her love for the arts is what spurred her to hone her talents as a digital designer, offering services to business owners and authors alike.

DocUmeant.net offers editing and writing services; DocUmeantDesigns.com, as you would guess, focuses on designs ranging from websites to book covers & layouts to buttons and business stationary needs; while DocUmeantPublishing.com's focus was begun with the Self-published author in mind. Now with ten years of experience in publishing she has built her success in the global community.

Ginger is a member of DesignFirms where she is a top rated designer, SPANpro (Small Publishers Association of North America), IBPA (International Book Publishers Association), DBW (Digital Book World), and is on the board of FAPA as VP Communications (Florida Authors and Publishers Association).

Most recently, Ginger was awarded for her generous contribution to Internet business while helping others achieve their goals in publishing and marketing. The Golden Mouse Award was presented to her by Women In e-Commerce on Oct 28, 2016. In 2012 she was awarded VIP membership to Covington's Who's Who and her publishing company, DocUmeant Publishing, was awarded the 2012 & 2016 New York Award in the Publishing Consultants & Services category by the U.S. Commerce Association (USCA). She recently won the 2015 Clearwater, FL Design Firm Award and has won book cover design awards and took home the silver medal for the *2015 Weird & Wacky Holiday Marketing Guide* from FAPA.

In her spare time she loves to do crafts of all sorts and sing. And yes, she is a little wacky at times too which keeps her fun and inspiring. Ginger lives in Florida where she works side-by-side with her husband, Philip, who is VP Editing for DocUmeant Publishing.

To contact Ginger whether for publish, design, or interviews you may reach her at ginger.marks@documeantdesigns.com or at 727-565-2130.

Additional Works by Ginger Marks

Visit Ginger's Amazon Author Central for more information or to purchase her books.

https://www.amazon.com/Ginger-Marks/e/B005ECOWD0/

The companion Playbook for the Annual *Weird & Wacky Holiday Marketing Guide* l will assist you in planning and tracking your holiday marketing success using the tools, tips, and resources found in the *Weird & Wacky Holiday Marketing Guide.*

- Easily plan and track your marketing
- Organized by month
- Room to write notes
- Track your success
- No expiration date! Start using any time.

Print: $12.97
Available at Amazon.com

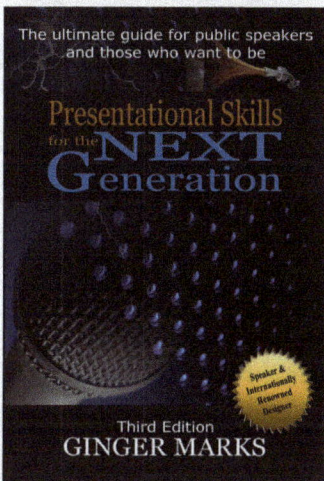

ISBN-13: 978-1937801779

Much has changed over the years in the public speaking arena. We have so many new and challenging tools at our disposal that we are no longer consigned to countless hours to travel from city to city to share our knowledge.

The Internet has opened the doors to people from all places and races. At the click of a button, you can share your information in many forms of multi-media. With the availability of hosting online conferences and collaborations in both text-only and A/V environments, as are offered by Skype Conference™, Hot Conference™ and desktop sharing applications such as Yugma™, as well as teleconferences, the modes and means are so plentiful that more and more savvy business owners are venturing into the public speaking arena.

It is a well thought out, concise, instructional manual written in a manner that all can comprehend. Within the contents of this guide, you will learn the skills necessary to enable you to present your information in such a way that you will capture the attention and hearts of your eager audience.

Available in Print $14.95

Also available in Digital $9.95

Print ISBN: 978-0-9788831-4-0
Digital ISBN: 978-0-9832122-7-0

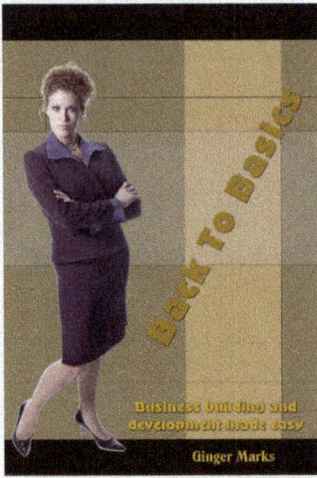

Back to Basics is a collection of articles designed to assist the new business owner to jump start their business or the seasoned profession to put the punch back into their chosen career. It begins with a two part series on the Nuts and Bolts of Business Building and continues from there to the ever important Marketing Basics. As marketing is an issue for each and every business owner no matter their business or circumstances this section is presented in three parts. This eBook comes in Kindle & PDF versions and at $2.99 it is a real bargain.

$2.99

Kindle Edition

Download: https://www.amazon.com/Back-Basics-Ginger-Marks-ebook/dp/B00A8SJ2D0

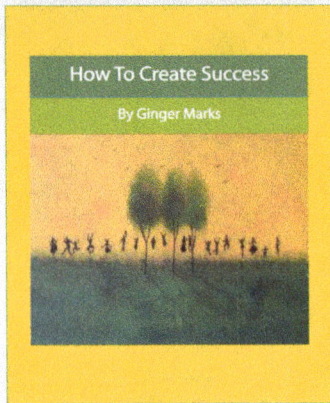

How To Create Success is the first eBook offering. Its bold colorful cover image entitled Jumping for Joy was designed by Amanda Tomasoa of Art by Amanda. The seven chapters contained within combine seven of the most highly rated articles written by Ginger at the time of publishing. One article "Contagious Influence" is currently the number one requested article and has been published in a magazine for writers titled 'Newbie News'. This is a free ebook and available for immediate download.

FREE Download: http://www.gingermarksbooks.com/PDFs/HowToCreateSuccess.pdf

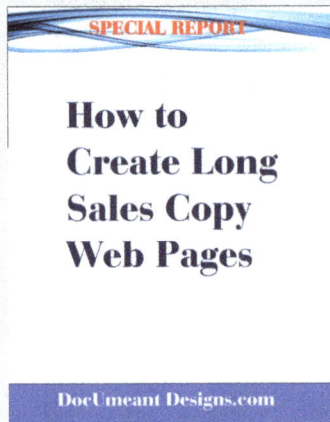

In this report you will learn how to create and effective *Long Sales Copy Web Page* and why you might need one. As you read through this report if you come to the conclusion that a *Long Sales Copy Web Page* is the right tool for your business, I highly recommend you use the company or individual with the working knowledge and integrity to create the site you need to get your important message across to your target market.

If you haven't a clue how to decipher who your target market is then that it the best place to start. Without this knowledge no matter how compelling you product or service message is, it will result in an ineffective campaign. This will end up costing you valuable time and money. Although this is beyond the context of this Special Report there are a myriad of resources available to you today online to help you along the way. As well, there are coaches who specialize in this area of expertise. Feel free to contact me and I will be happy to point you in the right direction.

To receive this FREE REPORT sign up for her monthly *Words of Wisdom eZine* here: http://www.gingermarksbooks.com/

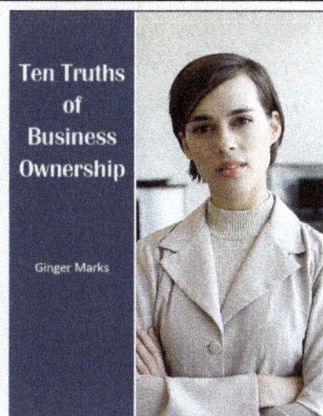

Discover the 10 truths every business owner should know. Knowing and applying these truths will aide you in achieving your dream of entrepreneurship.

To receive this eBook along with Ginger Marks' report *How to Create Long Sales Copy Web Pages* sign up for her monthly *Words of Wisdom eZine* her: http://www.gingermarksbooks.com/.

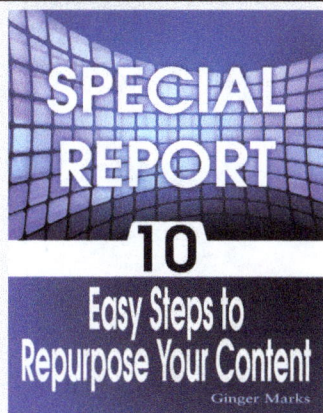

Get your copy of Ginger's Free Special Report: *10 Easy Steps to Re-purpose Your Content.* This is the insider's view of how the Complete Library of Entrepreneurial Wisdom came about. With the information you will garner in this Special Report, you too can quickly and easily create your very own new money maker.

Download: http://clewbook.com/

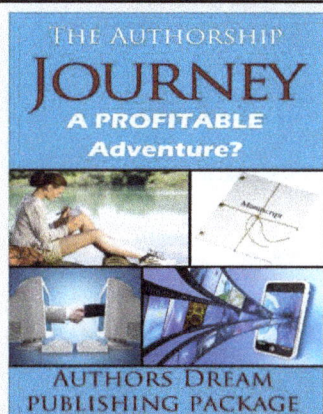

The journey to authorship is a road few travel. Find out how you too can traverse the challenges that lie ahead and come out on top. Advice from leading experts in the field.

$0.99

Kindle Edition

Download: https://www.amazon.com/ Authorship-Journey-profitable-adventure-ebook/dp/B00F8O5Z5S/

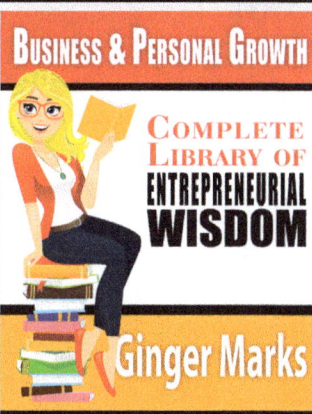

The *Complete Library of Entrepreneurial Wisdom* covers business basics, including how to and how not to start your business; marketing; marketing design, which is a topic rarely covered; writing, which covers technical, practical, as well as, marketing aspects to writing; and life reflections, such as planning for emergencies and disasters—both natural and man-made.

With over 150, power-packed, articles to choose from, the busy entrepreneur has at their fingertips, bite-sized training lessons to help them on their success journey. There is so much information packed into this book that it could well be the only book on core business issues that you will ever need.

$9.97 Kindle

$32.95 Hardcover

$24.95 Paperback

Hardcover ISBN: 978-1937801380

Paperback ISBN: 978-1494928292

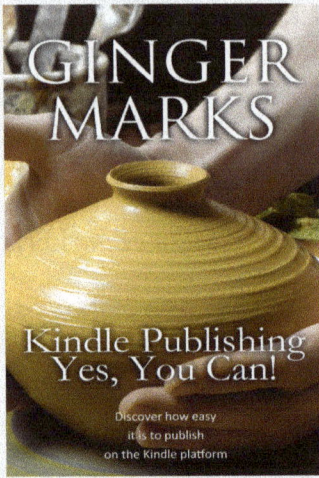

Publishing your ebook on Kindle doesn't guarantee your book will look the way you intended it to. Even using the Kindle generation tools can result in an ebook that isn't laid out the way you created it. In *Kindle Publishing, Yes You Can,* Ginger Marks, publisher and designer, explains in easy terms exactly what you need to do and how to create an ebook on Kindle that you will be proud to call your own.

$2.99 Kindle Edition

Available on Amazon.com at: https://www.amazon.com/Kindle-Publishing-Yes-You-Can-ebook/dp/B00KSQDTAY/

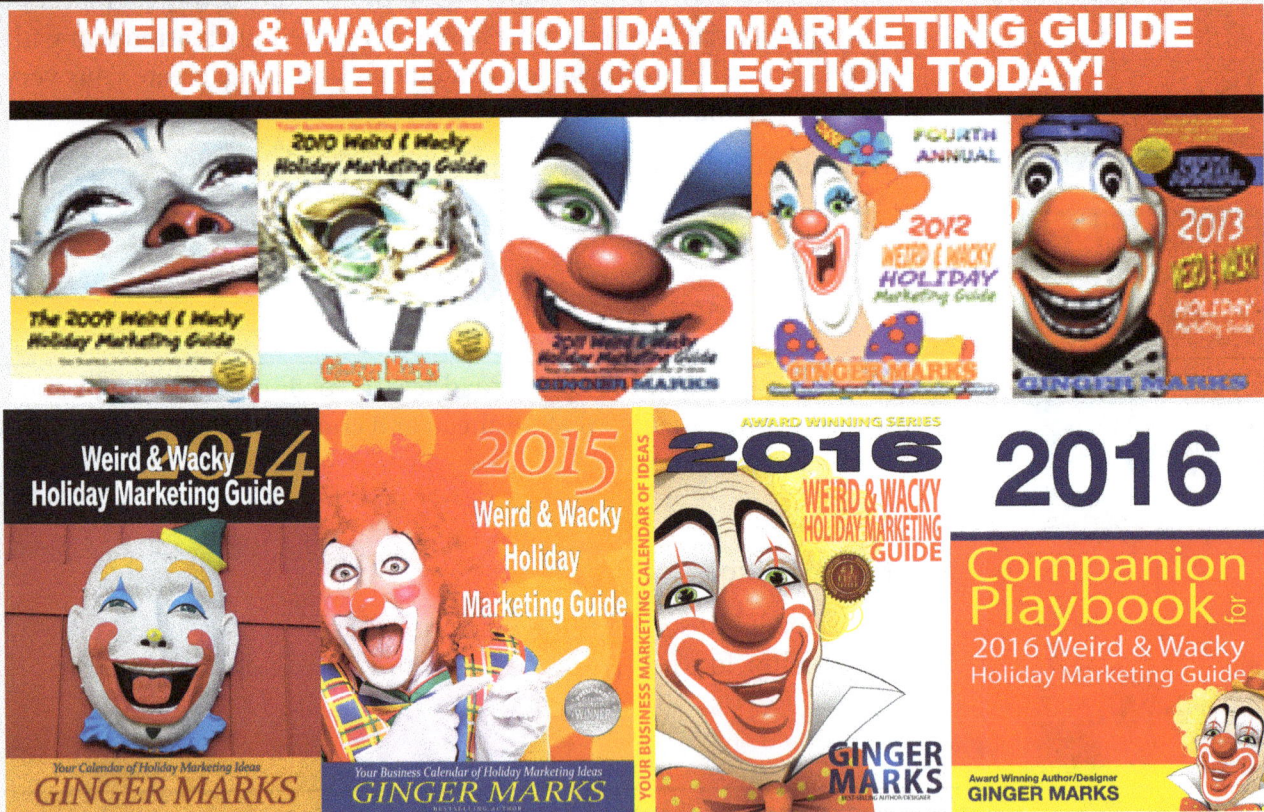

www.ingramcontent.com/pod-product-compliance
Lightning Source LLC
Chambersburg PA
CBHW062045090426

42740CB00016B/3021